FINDING CONNECTIONS

FINDING CONNECTIONS

P. J. Kavanagh

Hutchinson
London Sydney Auckland Johannesburg

This edition first published in 1990 by
Hutchinson

Century Hutchinson Ltd
20 Vauxhall Bridge Road, London SW1V 2SA

Century Hutchinson Australia (Pty) Ltd
20 Alfred Street, Milsons Point, Sydney NSW 2061, Australia

Century Hutchinson New Zealand Limited
PO Box 40–086, Glenfield, Auckland 10, New Zealand

Century Hutchinson South Africa (Pty) Ltd
PO Box 337, Bergvlei, 2012 South Africa

British Library Cataloguing in Publication Data
Kavanagh, P. J. (Patrick Joseph), *1931–*
    Finding connections
    1. Australasia. Description & travel
    I. Title
    919′.04

ISBN 0–09–173750–5

Set in Baskerville by Speedset Ltd, Ellesmere Port
Printed and bound in Great Britain by
Mackays of Chatham PLC, Kent

For Terence, Kevin Joseph, Siobhan, Cornelius, Bruno, and the descendants

Acknowledgements

Acknowledgements are due to the following books which have been of great assistance: *A History of Tasmania*, Lloyd Robson; *The Irish in Australia*, Patrick O'Farrell; *Churches and People of Australia and New Zealand, 1800–1930*, H. R. Jackson; *The Story of New Zealand*, W. H. Oliver; *Modern Ireland, 1600–1972*, R. F. Foster; *The Fatal Shore*, Robert Hughes; *Crossing the Gap*, C. J. Koch; *Down Home*, Peter Conrad. The author would also like to thank the following people for their generous help: Mr and Mrs Michael Courtney, C. J. Koch, Annette MacArthur Onslow, Father Terry Southerwood, Father Ernest Simmons, Ross Smith, Geoffrey Stillwell, Ken Scadden, Diane Wilson, Colleen Williams, Sunny Amey, David Garland, Andrew and Tina Kavanagh, Alec Burns, Michael Purcell, Dr Neutsch, Iain Macdonald, Robert Cotterall, Father Philip Caraman and Anne Rand; also the patient staffs of the Local History Archives in Launceston and Hobart.

Catholic nationalist culture continued to emphasize a coherent, commercialistic, self-sufficient nation; emigration was not interpreted as a rational, individualistic alternative, but as evidence of British disruption of the Irish way of life. A race-memory of exploitation, oppression and banishment flourished long after these concepts had become anachronistic; the memory of 'home' was perceived in the imagination as it had been when the emigrants (or their parents) had left.

R. F. Foster, *Modern Ireland 1600–1972*

a self-indulgent communal morbidity

D. N. Doyle

But spirits are not commonly perceptible or effective unless they have bodies, and no religion can live long without the codes, the guidance and the outward solidity of a church. True, the spirit may be overcome by the body; the church may miserably collapse under the dead load of its own tradition; yet there can never be a lasting faith without substance or without its appropriate doctrine, legend, rules, rituals and architecture.

C. E. Vulliamy, *John Wesley*

Contents

Prologue

The Croppie Grave

It was a bright spring evening in Carlow. A capless man in a frayed cardigan leaned on the parapet of the bridge over the river Barrow, watching the swans, watching the river flow past the maltings. What struck me about the man was that although he was looking, and had chosen a place in the still town where there were things to watch, because they moved – water, birds – he did not appear to be watching at all, was just slumped, thinking perhaps, or bored. Though I saw from the corner of my eye that he moved his head slightly as I passed, watching me from the corner of his. I mention the cardigan because his discreet awareness of my passing made me aware of my English jacket and tweed hat.

I was on my way to the Croppie Grave at the edge of town. Three men sat on the steps of the Sacred Heart Community Hall, the small houses on the far bank were eighteenth century, some perhaps early nineteenth, set next to dilapidated rural buildings that were once barns or stables. In the midst of a new housing estate, enclosed by a neat chain, white-painted, was the green mound.

> To the memory of six hundred and forty
> *United Irishmen*
> who fell in Tullow Street
> 25 May 1798

They were Irishmen, but were they italicised, and United?

They were misgoverned, misled, confused. The Rising of 1798 gave occasion to most kinds of brutality, legal and illegal, from those that rose and from those that suppressed; more, for obvious reasons, from the latter. The Croppies were so called, derisively, because of their presumed connection with the French Revolutionary fashion of cutting the hair short. Michael Farrell was a United Irishman, around on that night, though not in Tullow Street – which is why he lived to tell the story forty years later – and he thought the rebels might as well have pinned labels on themselves: 'The graceful locks, so much prized before, were shorn in an instant and a young man did not think he would be considered polite or in any degree fashionable if he did not display a pair of large ass's ears and bared to the very skull, as if he had a fit of the scald.' He says they did it to vex the magistrates, and therefore it is a comparatively innocent picture Farrell paints of Carlow before the rising. After it came the pitch-caps, set on fire on top of the cropped heads, the floggings and the hangings, and things were changed.

A few years before, I know I would have been wholly on their side: poor people armed with pikes against authority armed with muskets; peasants against oppressive landlords, Catholics against expropriating Protestants. But now those oppositions refused to come easily. Perhaps authority merely has to preserve order? This question, in such a place, startled and distressed me.

So I asked myself what had happened to me, imperceptibly over the years, asked the bones in the mound – children playing round it, a small dog venturing under its chain-link fence – conscious again of my English clothes.

As I walked back over the bridge an arm descended in front of me, like a railway signal falling. It belonged to Alec Burns, retired barber, and he wheeled his bicycle alongside.

'Did you notice the three trees on the grave? Look, you can see them above the roofs. See? A mother had three sons killed there that night. She didn't know they were there, didn't know where they were. Then a dove came in through the window and landed on her kitchen table and she knew they were dead. So when they were all covered over she planted three trees there, with a spoon.'

I liked the dove, liked the spoon.

'An American from Kentucky came over here, bored a hole in one of the trees. It was the right age. So he hired a plane and dropped a wreath on the grave.'

Legend, superstition, sentiment, help to make up the mythologies of historical Ireland, perhaps deepest rooted abroad, and they are not all untrue: that slaughter happened.

'It wasn't a *battle*, it was a massacre; no one on the government side was hurt. And there were Catholic militia among the troops, Catholic killing Catholic.'

He had a key to the little museum and let us into it. Inside was a piece of the trap-door of the scaffold on which more than two hundred had stood, in Carlow alone, in the weeks that followed the rising. There were playbills featuring an Edwardian comedian who had lived in the town; in one case were the cut-throat razors and mugs, impedimenta of Alec Burns's mystery, and in another were little crosses made from the wood taken from the coffin of a local priest, Father Maher. 'He cared for the poor people. When they moved him after seventy years his coffin was as good as the day it was nailed together. All the others were rotted in pieces.'

What all the exhibits had in common was that they came from people who did not have much. The priest whose coffin had not decayed would have had to care for those people in a political sense as well as pastorally, because the land was rich, the poverty unnecessary. (I discovered afterwards that he was a relation of mine.)

Why did I put that sentence in parenthesis? The discovery was the sort of exhibit I had hoped to find and hoped might add together and answer a question: the one raised by the dove and the spoon, which had moved me, as had the museum, more than its English equivalent would have done. I had felt a connection with it, and now found I had one, in Father Maher.

But I had also just caught myself wondering, for the first time, whether English authority could have behaved any differently towards the rebels. Had I, therefore, after three generations of my family outside Ireland, at last put down roots into the presuppositions of English authority? The question gave rise to a bigger one, which concerns millions of us, of many races: How long can we, should we, cling to old roots before we put down new ones?

In order to try to answer this it seemed necessary to go back in time. Twenty-five years before, I had gone back a little way and written a book, called *The Perfect Stranger*, because I wanted to try to make sense of the sudden death of my wife; sense for myself and, I hoped, in a general way for others. I was still trying to do this, and even as a part of that continuing attempt, which after all is reasonable – a wish to make sense of the world – I now wanted to go further back, and try to disentangle historical strands which had become confused, were confusing me.

A journey like that needs a starting-point, so I was in Carlow in search of a great-grandfather whose names I share. Perhaps I had chosen him for that reason, because names have power. The best Irish songs and poems move us because they name the girl, the hero, the traitor; they always insist on the particular, the date, the name, the place.

1

Carlow

In New Zealand some of my great-grandfather Patrick
Kavanagh's descendants believe that he came from Borris
House in County Carlow, the home of the chieftains of the
Kavanagh clan, ancient kings of Leinster, etc. No proof of this
has been discovered. Even the record of his date and place of
birth is missing. This legend, and the absence of any information, together with a sense of 'Irishness', undefined, had
clearly interested me for a long time, because years ago I put
some of it into a poem, after a visit to Borris. Also in the poem is
a story that Andrew Kavanagh, present head of the Kavanagh
clan, told:

Borris House, Co. Carlow

Ancestor-hunting: an interest as sudden
As middle age. As though I thought a chain
Of farmers, post office keepers, castle holders,
Bog kings, knackers, farmers' workers, traitors,
Clanked at my heel. And I did find one'

Great-grandfather, an old grandee or a great
Liar . . . French Jacobins making thought a thing to fear
What did they do, those summits of others' labour
Behind high walls, the nearest speakable neighbour
Sodden, impassable Irish miles away? In 'Ninety Eight.

Some flogged the blacksmiths; busy, essential men
With a ring of lingering magic round their craft.
Here ten were chained to the wine-cellar walls in dark
– The benches they sat on crumble away to cork –
And out of the ten, for death, one was chosen.

Perhaps he had made pikes for the Rebellion.
Perhaps not. Examples must be made, possessions held.
Perhaps. In recent years, over a bottle of wine,
The Rate Assessor faced the heir, his business done:
'Your ancestor', he said, 'killed one of mine . . .'

That was a just fight, cruelly put down.
The wall still stands, the length of the little town,
Whichever side of it, twenty years later, he was born
An embattled grandee, or great liar. There isn't a man
But knows both titles privately his own.

This was written long before I found in New Zealand that
Patrick Kavanagh is not recorded to have made such a claim,
and was therefore not 'a great liar', although he almost
certainly came from a farm on the Borris estate, or from the
estate itself. My father, his grandson, had hardly ever spoken
about his past in New Zealand, and when I grew curious
fended me off with jokes. It was through jokes that he made his
living and kept us fed. I suppose my first curiosity began about
1940 when I was nine and he was writing the radio show *Itma*,
which was becoming famous.

His silence and his jokes left me, I felt, in an odd position.
The fathers of my middle-class contemporaries were doctors or
solicitors or something with a name to it, and I seemed to
belong to no 'class' at all. They had uncles and aunts with
similar professions and houses, whereas most of my relations
were unknown, in New Zealand, or had been killed in the Great
War. As for houses, I had moved from furnished place to place

because of the Second World War, with my mother and a father who lived from hand to mouth by making jokes, which did not seem a 'profession' to me. Because of this my schoolfellows expected me to make jokes. Also, because of my name, I was thought of as 'a wild Irishman'. On top of this was my Roman Catholicism; at that early school I think I was the only one.

None of this was sad or painful, but it gave me the notion that my path was to be different from theirs: 'a wild Irishman' who had never been to Ireland, a Roman Catholic in a Protestant country, with a colonial clown for a father. (It was only later that I admired the way he stood outside the English pre-occupation with property and class.) At the time I reckoned I could live with this by making a virtue of distinctiveness. You invented yourself, the way you wanted to be, and you invented the world, the way you chose to see it, as truthfully as you could: you evolved a 'style'. What I came to lean on, at first unconsciously, was poetry and the Catholic form of Christianity, because both were 'classless' and both were a combination of invention, style and truth.

Nevertheless, this sense of belonging nowhere (by no means rare, which is why it is worth writing about) must have bothered me more than I realised. It was even a sense of not quite belonging to the world at all, which was of course encouraged by my Roman Catholic education – though I did not notice it having that effect on many of my schoolfellows. When I came to do my National Service (in an 'Irish' regiment, of course) I immediately volunteered to fight in Korea. This was partly a desire for travel and adventure. But when I reached Japan I volunteered so often to be sent to the fighting battalion, and when I was sent to Korea in charge of War Correspondents, I went so frequently to visit that battalion in the line, urgently to press my claims, eventually getting my way, there seems something odd about such persistence. Then, when I found myself under fire at very close quarters, expecting imminent death, it was all a long time ago, but I do not remember feeling fear. It is easy to remember the past wrongly, but it does seem clear that I did not particularly want to live: it is as though the complexities and confusions of not belonging anywhere, of not knowing who I was, were too much, and I wanted to hand back my ticket. Yet I *did* know who I was. If I was not in love with life I was, I believe, unusually lively. What I could not find was, in Carson McCullers's phrase, 'the we of me'.

Yet I believed without question that it existed. When I eventually found it, and met Sally in 1953, two years after my experience in Korea, it was all much more complicated and exciting than that apparently sentimental formula, nevertheless it was true, a confirmation of faith, and a rescue; I wanted to live very much indeed. We married in 1956 and when Sally died of polio in 1958 I seemed to be back where I started – but not quite. I had been shown something beautiful and fundamentally simple, had seen faith in a possibility justified, and it was the responsibility of the rest of my life to keep faith with that.

A lifetime later this had left me with some tricky disconnections hanging loose in the attic of my mind, and it was time to consider these, or so I thought as I looked up at the worrying tangle of wires that criss-crossed the sky above the main street of Carlow, 'the Athens of Leinster'. I could smile at the epithet, but I felt unusually at home there.

What I liked about it was what made many of my English friends impatient: the unorganised friendliness; respect for passing passions of anger or enthusiasm; an ability to waste time; an unselfconsciousness about religious observance (a woman coming out of a little chapel opposite the hotel, absently crossing herself as she continued with her shopping, pleasantly reminded me of this); no pressure or stratification of class.

Nevertheless an English irritation with the derivatives of some of these things was what I had felt at the Croppie Grave:

an impatience with an insurrection incompetently led, with dreams that had no practical foundation, with a national self-pity that found expression in poems and ballads that could distil poison. In other words, I had thought like an Englishman (not wrongly, but uncomfortably), had met Alec Burns with his tales of doves and spoons and undecaying wooden coffins and had felt at home.

But why should I not feel at home, now that I knew about Father Maher? Already other things had been discovered. I was standing not twenty yards from eighteenth-century Brown Street where Patrick Kavanagh had lived before his marriage and for a while after it, until he took his wife and child to Van Diemen's Land in 1841. The address was on his marriage certificate. Why should it not feel a homely place when my forefathers had been in it, or around it, just about for ever?

Here he had married a girl called Margaret Paul, whose uncle became Cardinal Cullen, and that, so far, was all I had been able to find out about Patrick. They were married in the cathedral, built in 1783, one of the first such buildings put up after the repeal of the Penal Laws. It towers above the town, and next to it is a vast seminary, Saint Patrick's, like an eighteenth-century palace. Margaret's brother James became a priest there. Perhaps at Saint Patrick's they would know about the Pauls, since the Kavanaghs were proving difficult to trace?

They did not; priests do not go in for family history. But they remembered James, because from New Zealand he had sent them their sanctuary lamp. In that country, in 1866, he had helped to establish his sister and brother-in-law, Margaret and Patrick; which is why, eventually, my father came to be born there. But all that was to be discovered later.

Now, in Saint Patrick's, I learned there were seventy student-priests, but room for two hundred. Was Catholicism on the wane, even in Ireland?

'We have enough for our purposes,' said Father McEvoy,

head on one side, watchful. 'England will have to find her own. Australia, New Zealand, those sorts of places.'

He was hinting that Ireland had done her bit in that respect, which it had. Even our parish priest in England had been trained here: Father O'Donnell, from Fermanagh. Thirty years in Gloucestershire had done nothing to anglicise his accent, so that his sermons were nearly incomprehensible. I had sometimes wondered if we should have loved him so much if we could have understood what he was saying. But what little we did understand was about love of God, the need we had to forgive each other, and ourselves. He was a good man, and firmly traditionalist. In fact, he was a one-man assault on the Second Vatican Council. If the Mass was to be in English, all right, but he made sure from his pronunciation of the English that it remained as mysterious as when it was in Latin. He had recently died; Father McEvoy was that day composing his obituary. I should have liked to have been able to tell Father O'Donnell that I had visited his seminary. Now, clearly, the supply of O'Donnells for export was drying up.

Father McEvoy told me of an organisation called 'Carlow Heritage', which sounded imposing, but to go in search of it was, as I had hoped, to be drawn into a web of Irish informalities and personal connections, which was part of the point of the search.

The man who ran it, Michael Purcell, would be in his shop; at his shop he had just gone out, would be back, would not, would be at 'the Scotch church'; everyone helpful, involved in the search for him. At the Scotch church he was not (the building itself a part of Carlow history, result of Protestant liturgical quarrels last century), but a passer-by said he would be in the hall behind the *Methodist* church opposite. Where also he was not – as why should he have been, for my convenience, dropped in for a moment from another world? But there were young people tidying up the grass outside it and one of them promised to get a message to him. Later, elsewhere in the town, the young man pulled up on his bicycle, said he was still looking. Later, in another part, someone unknown called out that he had been found, gave a time and a place to meet him. Already, after a couple of days in Carlow, I seemed to know more people than we knew in our local English town after many years.

In the afternoon he was found in the Methodist hall, volubly at work, striding among boxes and files on trestle tables, surrounded by bored young people on some government training scheme, himself the sole energiser of the endeavour. He had set himself the task of compiling a list of births, marriages and deaths for the whole of County Carlow, which had never been done before, and the records were in disorder. Most of the boxes contained thousands of questions about their antecedents from Australia, Canada, the United States; he seemed to be trying to tidy up a considerable part of the Irish diaspora, helped by a small government grant. He was nearly overwhelmed, but not quite, so fascinated by the whole vast business had he become.

On me the sight of that room, and the work going on inside it, had a double effect. The questions I was asking had already brought me into contact with a side of Ireland I did not know, which was good. But facts were going to be hard to come by, which was not good, and I was searching for something even more elusive, for the source of certain feelings, in myself and others; and this was hardly to be found in that room.

About Patrick Kavanagh Purcell could give no help until he had mastered the whole county. He was almost certainly not born in Carlow town. He was married there to Margaret Paul, whose mother was Ellen Cullen: that was on Purcell's list. Then he noticed that Margaret's father was called Richard: 'Richard Paul . . . *Richard Paul*! I know his house. I've written about it. It's in Tullow Street! He was a big man here. Richard Paul!'

That was encouraging, in a way, but finding, as I knew I would, births, marriages and deaths a barren ground for my quest – though wherein else lay the story of a place, I did not know, save in imagination and invention, which because of my own emotional pull towards Ireland I did not trust – I went outside for a smoke. There, sitting on the steps in the thin spring sunshine, were some of the young assistants, girls and boys politely bemused by the dustiness of their task, their lives lying fresh before them; yet this obsessive journey backward was all that life offered for the moment. I was followed out of the hall by a retired Irish journalist who helped Purcell occasionally. We were about of an age, the right one for delving, unlike the young people on the steps nearby. We lit up together, I with relief, for the size of the task inside had reminded me of the probable frustration of my own.

'Is he any good at it?' I asked.

'He's a kind of genius, an untutored genius.' My companion was clear and amused in his admiration.

The town lay pleasantly around us, little changed since Patrick's day. 'Why should anyone want to leave this place, before the Famine, with his wife and small child, to go to a gaol, Van Diemen's Land, on the other side of the world?'

'Was the poor man deported?' The question was full of sympathy. It would not have been asked in that way in England. But I knew already that he was not a convict. In terms of tracing him it would have been simpler if he had been. 'Was he anything to do with the militia?' It was only afterwards that I wondered if I had misunderstood that question, for I answered no, he had not been a soldier.

But these are still delicate matters in Ireland. What came to mind later was what Alec Burns had said the previous evening: that it was not a battle, it was a massacre; that there were Catholics in the militia, Catholics killing Catholics.

The Rising of 1798 is sometimes simplified into a tale of oppressed Catholics against Protestant oppressors. The grievances were real, but the over-simplification is a part of the Irish historical mythology that can prove so dangerous, especially when exported. (Shortly before I wrote these words I heard that Mayor Koch of New York returned home from a visit to Northern Ireland and announced that the British army was there to keep the peace. Within hours, reminded that 10 per cent of his constituents were of Irish descent, he uttered an urgent disclaimer: Sorry, what he really meant was that it was an *army of occupation*. Irish history, or versions of it, is thus brooded over and distorted.) Few in Ireland, I would guess, still feel the bitterness or would subscribe wholly to the myth.

Nevertheless, inside that Methodist hall, they had been astonished, as they dug deeper, to discover the extent of the reprisals after '98: confiscations and executions on small evidence or none, 'even of the gentry', they said, in wonder. The bitterness of that would surely have been in the air of Carlow when Patrick was born, around 1818, and would have lingered, probably until 1841, when he left. If Patrick Kavanagh came from 'the big house' at Borris (as estate worker, bastard, or whatever) it was not unlikely that he might have been part of some government militia, therefore unpopular and best out of the place. It was equally likely that he was on the other side, unpopular with his masters, and therefore also best away.

2

Father Maher

Whatever his allegiances, Patrick certainly married into a
family that was on the wrong side, as far as the English
authorities and Church of Ireland landowners were concerned,
although it was not on the side of rebellion either.

A newcomer to this sort of investigation learns at once that
almost anything can lead to a discovery. In that Methodist hall
I casually picked up a local history magazine, *Carloviana*, and
found an article by Professor Donal McCartney about Father
James Maher.

From the government point of view he was a turbulent
priest, a part, says McCartney, 'of what has been called the
Catholic clerical aristocracy of Kildare and Leighlin – the
Mahers, Morans, Cullens. His nephew and close friend,
Archbishop Cullen, was Ireland's first Cardinal and his
grand-nephew Archbishop Moran was also a Cardinal (in
Australia). His immediate relations formed the hard core of the
rising educated Catholic middle-classes who looked after the
numerous new churches and convents that were beginning to
dot the 19th century Irish landscape.'

Here, at last, was a series of connections. Although only by
marriage did they have anything to do with Patrick, they had to
do, by blood, with me. My great-great-grandmother was Ellen
Cullen, the archbishop's sister, who married Richard Paul,
and therefore I was related to Father Maher, who was Cullen's
uncle. (One can only take so much of this, and there will be no
more.) It was important for me to spell it out to myself because,

for the first time, I knew that my sense of being Irish and my discomfort with aspects of English authority were not merely sentimental, but had some identifiable historical roots. Father Maher and others like him were outside the plans and assumptions of the England-dominated, Protestant-dominated Ireland of their time, as I was not at home with much that was English in my day. Priests worked from a different spiritual starting-point; were a part of the creation of the new Ireland that slowly, round about the 1840s, was coming into being. In that article, so casually come upon, I recognised the source of the ethos in which I was brought up a hundred years later. I now knew why I liked this place and liked these people.

Father Maher was one of the priests who stilled agrarian uprising with his own authority; though not for the sake of the gentry, or the government, whom this exercise of power made uneasy. They felt it was they who should quell violence, not the priests. 'But', Professor McCartney says, 'that battle had been fought. Aristocracy, whether Catholic or Protestant, was retreating, unevenly, it is true, before the advances of democracy, and in the diocese of Kildare and Leighlin, it was men like Bishop Doyle and his friend and ally Father Maher whose influence mattered to an increasing extent.' They were giving dignity back to the native Irish.

He became a first-class pest, endlessly composing fierce pamphlets in his study at Saint Patrick's, splendidly quoting Grattan: 'The peasant is born without an estate: he is born with hands and no man has a natural right to the labour of those hands unless he pays him.'

During the Famine in the mid-1840s various evangelising societies from England made a concerted attempt to convert Ireland to Protestantism. It was a crusade with bribes: the converted were promised food and clothes. (The wit of ordinary men is everywhere equal to such occasions. Those who converted were called 'soupers'.) Maher thundered against this advantage-taking, particularly objecting to the way 'fanatical women of unsteady minds and ill-regulated piety collected large sums of money and formed themselves into committees giving thanks to God that they were thus privileged in spreading the gospel light in many dark and remote corners of Ireland. Good heavens, is it possible they are so blinded as not to perceive the frightful iniquity of their proceedings?' He ungallantly called them 'the faded beauties of the metropolis', holding what he called the old-fashioned notion of St Paul that a woman's place is in the home, where her influence is invaluable. Professor McCartney tries to absolve him of sexism: 'A man, however, whose two sisters and eighteen nieces were nuns, also believed that 19th century women might choose to devote themselves to God.' Good Heavens (as Father Maher might say), two sisters and eighteen nieces! What sort of a family was this that I was connected with? (And small wonder I had so few relations.) Reading more of the thunders of Father Maher, I was also reminded of how embarrassed I had sometimes been by my father's over-use of alliteration as a comic device. Perhaps that ran in the family – as well a priests and nuns – for Maher declares himself determined 'to fairly expose the folly and fanaticism, the fraud and falsehood'.

Those were bad times, and there was a battle to be fought, as Father Maher surely saw it, for Ireland's soul. But it is difficult to accept the violence of the rhetoric he used, for we know that the seed he planted still grows. (It is important to remember, in extenuation, the power he was up against.) 'Centuries of persecution have not appeased the foes of our name and race. . . . No power on earth ever persecuted a subject people so long, so inexorably, so remorselessly with such blind fury, and senseless hate, as imperious England has persecuted this unhappy land.' We may wince, but we were not there, we have not seen what he saw, he was not mad. Even now, loving England as I do, I feel myself responding; there is in me an ineradicable sympathy with Ireland.

Michael Farrell, the young United Irishman who somehow survived the '98 Rising in Carlow, describes what happened to his native place in the forty years that followed. He is doubtless a biased source, but what source is not? History is a matter of atmosphere, as well as of facts, and his sense of his native place, at about the time Patrick left it, would have been more or less the same as Father Maher's and perhaps Patrick's. Farrell writes with prescience; he warns of a greater hunger to come, three years before the Great Famine in 1845.

In the short space of about forty years [after 1798], from being a nation of honest, industrious and wealthy tradesmen and dealers of every description, headed by honourable noblemen and gentlemen, we have become a nation of swindlers, bankrupts and beggars. A nation possessing a soil and a climate, producing every necessary of life as abundantly as any other spot on the globe, and every province, every county, every town in it producing its thousands of human beings in a state of starvation, men able and willing to labour for their bread, and no one to give them employment, and at the same time thousands upon thousands of acres of land lying waste and uncultivated – what do our rulers mean? Do they mean to thin the human race, to murder them by famine? There is no doubt about it. There is no use in mincing the matter or in calling things by any other than their right names; thousands upon thousands have died of starvation in Ireland these thirty years past and thousands are little better than dying of it at the moment, though it is the month of October 1842, but how they will be next spring and summer when provisions are always dear and scarce God alone who gives plenty to the birds only knows.

Farrell's idea that the miseries of Ireland were the result of a government plot, even an attempt at genocide, is a constant strain in some Irish thinking. Farrell (and others) believed that

William Pitt wanted the rising, connived at it, in order to be able to identify and kill off the dissidents and have an excuse to abolish the Irish Parliament (which abolition took place). Three generations later, the socialist James Connolly had found by 1916 (when he was executed) that he could not make his countrymen reconcile their nationalism with his Marxism; he put it down to their 'atavism', but also to 'the devilish ingenuity of the master class'.

One of the greatest sources of grievance in Father Maher's time was the Church of Ireland, to which tithes had to be paid by the 90 per cent of the people who did not belong to it. He was of course fond of quoting Edmund Burke on the subject: 'Don't talk to me of its being a religion: it is a wholesale robbery'; and Macaulay: 'Of all institutions now existing in the civilised world, the Established Church of Ireland is the most absurd and indefensible.' But he lived to read in the London *Times*, quoted by Professor McCartney, that 'its bishops received the incomes of Prime Ministers for superintending dioceses containing no more Protestants than were to be found in an ordinary London parish . . . It preserved the ascendancy of class over class, that worst mischief in Irish politics. It was one of the grounds of the vague discontent in the hearts of the Irish peasantry.' (The great strength of the Catholic church in Ireland was that it had never been associated with a ruling class.) Father Maher died in 1874 and had seen by that time the disestablishment of the Church of Ireland in 1869, and a beginning to the dismantling of the landlord system by the Land Act of 1870. He had fought on these fronts and on others, for his people, and those little wooden crosses made out of his first coffin suggest that they appreciated this; even perhaps, at one time, that a small cult grew up round his name. Alec Burns said he always drew people's attention to those crosses in the museum, as he had drawn mine.

Whether I would have liked to have lived in the priest-ruled Ireland Father Maher helped to create I cannot tell, being

English, born in England. My father had an affection for it, but he too lived in England. Now, that Ireland no longer exists, or not in the same way. If I had to choose I would prefer the authority of priests (up to a point) to that of lawyers, or of secular ideologues. The Reformation did a great deal for the upper-middle class of England but not much for anyone else, that I have heard. At any rate, this view of English history, I realise, is now buried too deep in my consciousness to be dug out. Even in England I received a kind of Irish-Catholic education, due to Father Maher and others like him, and their effect on my father and his father and, for all I knew, his father too, the elusive Patrick.

3

Leighlinbridge

Automatically spelling my name to the receptionist at the Carlow hotel, as I would do in England, I saw she had written it down correctly before I had finished. This was the home of the name, as Gloucestershire, where I live, is not. There are no Kavanaghs on the war memorials and gravestones of Gloucestershire. Awareness of this, over the years, was one of the reasons I was briefly back in Carlow.

There would be plenty of Kavanaghs in the street outside the hotel, but none descended from Patrick Kavanagh, who had left that street, or a side-turning off it twenty yards down the road, a hundred and fifty years before. I was looking for him –in a way. The imprecision was intentional; I was looking for a certain sort of 'Irishness' and some understanding of how it can survive over generations out of Ireland; looking for a sense of its value, or lack of it.

For me this was central, because it was a puzzle in myself that I hung on to, making my English friends shake their heads, my immaterialisms dismaying them. They would have teased me with Douglas Hyde's words – 'the piety of the Irish Gael, who sees the hand of God in every place, in every time, in everything' (like the Greeks in Homer) – and I would have agreed with a justice in their tease; but their pragmatism chilled me, although I envied the daylight of their logic.

Yet Father Maher I understood, as perhaps they would not. He might not have understood me, for I too was pragmatic and English, protestant even, in the sense that I believed a man's relation with God is a private matter, but I understood his drift, which was other-worldly yet within the world, an inside-outsider. He had followed that drift and fought his fight in this air, this town, in a way no one had drifted or fought, effectively, in England for four hundred years. To try to do so there was to be thought backward-looking, like the Oxford Movement, like William Morris and the Pre-Raphaelites (whose return was to the Middle Ages, with the Christian spine left out); even those who admire and quote G. K. Chesterton believe his Christendom-centred interpretation of English history to be absurd. The trade unions, initially Christian-inspired, soon left out any mention of supernatural justice.

It was therefore reasonable (logical) to feel cheered and companioned in Carlow, because of the link with Maher; and to be pleased to find him, for his time, in the political avant-garde, because in England I had been made to feel irretrievably lost in old outmoded superstitions. This genealogical search, diffident as it was, undertaken in doubt as to whether it was any decent way to find out about the past – what one's own great-grandfather did or did not do, was or was not – had already thrown up a thin line of connection which mitigated my resigned, almost automatic, sense of intellectual isolation. Let the amateur investigation therefore continue, I thought. Professionals had been asked if they could find out anything about Patrick but they could not. Andrew Kavanagh at Borris could not. What, then, could I discover about the Cullens, the family of Patrick's mother-in-law, who were made cardinals and the like?

A look in Carlow Library was enough to show that Cardinal Cullen was a political and ecclesiastical potentate and a hardliner. It was his definition of papal infallibility that had been accepted by the Vatican, and this had more or less put paid to the conversions to Catholicism from the Oxford Movement – few Englishmen could accept a dogma that looked so irrational. Cullen filled the newly founded church organisation in Australasia with his like-minded placemen, many of them relations, and Cardinal Newman could only look on appalled at this Irish takeover, fearful Cullen might do the same in Scotland, in England even. It seems the products of the Oxford Movement did not approve of this Irish movement, and this cheered me too, because there is something too aesthetic, too 'gentlemanly', about those Victorian Romanists. I preferred Maher.

Alec Burns said there was a butcher called Cullen at Leighlinbridge who kept a history of his family.

It is a quiet little village now, on the banks of the river Barrow, once busy, for there are eighteenth-century warehouses next to the water and what must have been a wharf. There is a ruined castle that was the barracks in 1798, in those days a place of dread to Michael Farrell. Now, next to it, an old grey horse grazed in a watermeadow studded with wild irises, flags, that had not yet opened, and grey wagtails caught flies neatly, just above the surface of the smooth water.

Mr Cullen, in his small shop on the bank, was not surprised I should wish to see his family tree, which he kept at home in a safe, and he would fetch it down when he went home for lunch.

A fingerpost pointed to 'Saint Lazarian's Holy Well'; I followed it up a hill and came upon Saint Lazarian's, a vast Church of Ireland edifice, locked, built against an older, crumbling church, now collapsed, mossy, with jackdaws nesting. The Catholic church, further along, was big and new and fairly ugly, like most new Catholic churches in Ireland. The compulsion to build, and build big, is a legacy from a time when they were not allowed to build at all. Whereas an original Irish church, like Cormac's chapel at Cashel, in the navel of Ireland, is my idea of the perfect church: small, intimate, abstractly decorated, like the idealised cell of a holy man.

The well was further on, and new tarmac was being laid on the approach to it. The spring had been enclosed with breeze-blocks, and within these, round the well-head, were carefully placed and surprising offerings, some of which had been there a long time: a piece of chocolate, paper clips, unburned match-sticks, a broken comb. I left an Irish penny. Saint Lazarian is unknown to any dictionary of saints I have looked at, although there were lazar-houses run by clergy (whose patron was Lazarus), but these were mostly in France (as in Gare Saint-Lazare). I asked the workmen who he or she was and, embarrassed, they 'had to confess' they did not know.

By this time Mr Cullen (my kinsman; it was pleasant to have discovered these remote cousinships; I realised I felt their absence in England) had returned from his lunch, reopened his shop and, after dealing with a customer, spread out the long handwritten scroll of his family tree along his counter. Against some of the names was 'Arrested 1798' and 'Killed 1798', but he did not draw attention to these. (Farrell speaks of sharing a cell with a Paul Cullen, whom he knew to be unconnected with the rising; nevertheless Cullen was taken out and hanged.) Every name on the scroll was a Cullen; presumably when Ellen Cullen married and became a Paul she was of no further interest. Perhaps all family trees are like that, otherwise they would become too complicated, and this one looked compli-cated enough. I did not examine it closely – I was surprised by the recoil of boredom it caused in me – any more than I looked closely, later, at the illuminated and vellum tree of the great family at Borris House ('You *do* give up easily!' said Tina Kavanagh). I would never be a genealogist; I was a fraud, in a way, pretending an interest in family trees, in anyone's, including my own. But I was also secretly pleased, because something was becoming clear.

It is not always easy to define the tiny spurt of fascination that can contain the seed of something very like love. It lay in the way those workmen said they 'had to confess' they did not know who Saint Lazarian was. The previous night I had bumped into a man who, when he was told I was a writer, said to me genially, 'I may be a bit inebriated, but I can't fockin' *read* modern books!' No workman in England would say he 'had to confess' he did not know something, no equivalent to my cheerful street-encounter would use the word 'inebriated' unselfconsciously. Of course it was not just those words, but thousands of flavours, gestures, incidents, that accumulate into an essence. I remembered the poet Peter Redgrove, on his first visit to Ireland, going into a shop to buy some string and coming out almost reeling with pleasure because he had been carefully asked whether he wanted 'string' or 'twine'. He had also turned to me in wonder, in the west of Ireland, after closely observing some families in an hotel: 'Is it my imagination, or do Irish families on holiday actually love each other?' All these tiny impressions, added up, do not make Ireland better than England but make it different, and it was this difference, which interested me, that had caused most of the trouble between the two countries: the English do not like differences in those who otherwise seem so like themselves – especially, of course, when those others seem less sensible, and on purpose. My delight in the difference, I realised, was a form of expiation for this. When I had irritated my English friends, and some Irish ones – who, from a man they regard as wholly anglicised, perhaps suspected a sort of 'nigger-loving' condescension – by drawing attention to these distinctions of speech and manner which add up to a different way of looking at the world, I had really been trying to suggest that instead of rejection of them, or a 'Paddyfying' of them, an enjoyment of these foreign colours would enlarge England. It was even possible, I thought (for Ireland goes to the head), that I was born to contribute a brick, however small, to a bridge between the two cultures; for two separate cultures they are. That was why I was in Ireland, and about to go chasing Irishness in Australia; not in order to look up family trees, but to mark the differences and try to explain them, not least to myself.

Nevertheless, there remained Richard Paul's house to look at, in Tullow Street. He was, I had to keep reminding myself, counting on my fingers, my great-great-grandfather – or one of them.

Tullow Street is where the rebels were trapped in 1798 and the massacre took place, 640 of them killed, according to the stone on the Croppie Grave. A priest had knelt in the roadway, imploring them not to go on. But no, they believed they had only to 'raise a shout' in Tullow Street for the town, the militia and enough of the soldiers to declare for them, and the place would be theirs. So they had been told.

It is a wide street of small, mostly eighteenth or early nineteenth-century houses. It narrows and is blocked off, more or less, by a much larger house of an unusual three storeys. That was my great-great-grandfather's. Anyone opposing the rebels, if they marched up that street, would use it as a block-house to fire from.

In any equivalent English town it would surely be possible to find out who was the owner of that house that night and what role he played (supposing such a killing had ever taken place in modern England); but Ireland is not like that. The army and the government were chiefly interested in themselves and the gentry. There is a sense in which to them 'the Irish' were undifferentiated. Even a merchant in a fairly large way of business, such as Richard Paul, would have his participation recorded only if he had conspicuously impeded or had been unusually helpful. Nor is it in the interests of any army to have its actions too closely examined.

A prosperous merchant would have had little to gain from rebellion, nor would Richard Paul's Catholicism have neces-sarily put him on the rebels' side. His wife's family, the Cullens, were certainly against republicanism. The church, mistrusting England as much as anybody, was not in favour of rebellions it could not control. There was an internal political struggle going on which the church won. In the mid-nineteenth century a firm hand, an Irish clerical one, fell on Ireland, and it was Cardinal Cullen's. Within a century it became in some ways a dead hand, stifling, and by the 1950s thoughtful Irish people, when they could, left the island because of this. Authority is always the problem, the extent and degree of it. It is needful, but how to prevent its excess? (This is the uncomfortable question raised by contemplation of that green mound at the edge of town.)

Michael Purcell remembered, as a boy, seeing 'Richard Paul, Maltster' written in fading paint on the front of that house. Attached to it are still the high, stone-built maltings that he used, with stables and a large turning-circle for the drays and horses. Purcell said there might still be sacks in there, with 'Richard Paul' written on them; he thought he had glimpsed some, years before, through the barred windows.

With the present owner of the maltings, Michael Doyle, who uses them as a storage place for his machines, I climbed the original ladders into the high-ceilinged lofts with their smooth wooden malting-floors, among winches and pulleys that would have been there in Richard Paul's day. There were no sacks.

Afterwards we stood outside and looked across at Doyle's large modern shop, which sold agricultural machinery, and could have been anywhere in Europe. Three eighteenth-century houses had been pulled down to make way for it. 'Economic necessity,' he said. He was ambitious, efficient in a Euro-Community way, indistinguishable from his English or German counterparts. Yet the Doyles had been on that corner for generations; his great-great-grandfather had been Richard Paul's neighbour and must have seen Patrick come a-courting. Perhaps the Pauls, if they had stayed, would have torn their maltings down and built a supermarket? It certainly seemed a selective search for 'Irishness' that I was making. Perhaps it was for an Irishness of mind, best preserved abroad?

After he left me I took photographs, a little forlornly. It was possible that my search was already too late, that Ireland was flattening out, like the rest of the world, becoming undifferentiated. It struck me as absurd, the photography – it always does. Nevertheless I perched among the parked cars and avoided the moving ones, hoping to find the best angle for those grim-looking buildings. I had come to look for the spirit of Patrick Kavanagh and had ended up taking photographs of the one-time *property* of his father-in-law. Well, Andrew Kavanagh, among whose ancestors Patrick was rumoured to be, could tell me nothing of him, nor could anyone else. Here, at least, was a fact.

The house, as has been said, blocks the end of Tullow Street, and after it the town peters out into garage forecourts, little factories with wire fences; a fairly desolate piece of the twentieth century after the bustling human proportions of the street itself. Then, as I snapped and jostled for position, I saw Andrew Kavanagh running along that nondescript stretch of wire and broken asphalt.

We stared at each other as astonished as we had been years before when we had come unexpectedly face to face on a deserted beach in a particularly underpopulated part of Connemara. It was as though we followed each other about: a man in search of his family, continually bumping into the man who was the head of that family (if my great-grandfather belonged to it). I felt almost furtive, tempted to hide the camera, unwilling to explain, as I had to, that I was photographing a forebear's house. He asked why I had not told him I was coming, and the reason for that was difficult to explain also. The legend of the family connection with his house, so deeply entrenched in New Zealand, had increasingly come to feel an embarrassment and a distraction. This was his world, and mine was different.

Now, questions more easily answerable than Patrick's ancestry were moving in my mind. 'Was the poor man deported?' I thought not, but now knew the difficulty of being sure of anything. What were his circumstances? To get any picture of him at all I had to know something of these, but I could find no clue. The historian Patrick O'Farrell makes the case that only the well-off went to Australia: 'All reports tell the same story: it was the "comfortable" farmers, those with "ample means", able to realise their assets, who were the emigrants.' Was Patrick one of these? Or was he poor? To what degree had he taken his Irishness with him abroad, for he seemed to have transmitted it to his son, his son to my father, and thence, in some form, to me? O'Farrell adds, disconcertingly: 'A corollary proposition is that emigration created a cultural and intellectual vacuum in which the destinies of Ireland lapsed into the hands of romantics, fools, poets and extremists with tenuous Irish connections, with disastrous effects on Irish history.' With my tenuous Irish connections, is that how my idea of Ireland had been formed – by romantics, fools, poets, and not by the Father Mahers, not by Patrick at all? I had been as little interested by the Euro-Doyle as he by me. Perhaps what I loved about Ireland was its picturesque plainness, its poorness? One thing to be said about this investigation, it was at least complicated. However, except when confronted by a family tree, I would not give up as easily as that. In order to get some sense of order into the tale, and look for the roots of Irishness, at least abroad, and still uncertain whether to put Irishness into inverted commas, I should have to follow Patrick to Van Diemen's Land.

4
Melbourne

The *Arab* has brought out a large number of immigrants, chiefly agricultural labourers, selected in England by the friends of those colonists to whom the servants were indentured, and shipped under the superintendence of Mr Dowling. There are 205 men, women and children. Three children died on the passage, and five were born on the *Arab*. In looking over the applications for a free passage sent to the Land and Emigration Commissioners, we were gratified to find that not one of the applicants had been in receipt of parish relief. Their robust healthy appearance reflects great credit on those who selected and those who have had care of them; and we have no doubt they will be found a valuable acquisition to the colony.

Allowing for the orotund period style, you need not listen hard to hear the patronising note in that account of the *Arab*'s arrival at Launceston, Tasmania, the sound of 'old' colonists putting new ones in their place: 'Their robust healthy appearance' – did they inspect their teeth and pinch their flesh, as they stood on the quay with their infants and bundles? As for the 'free passage' investigations, quite well-to-do migrants sometimes travelled as cheaply as they could, as some always do, for obvious reasons. There is little to be learned about the circumstances of Patrick on that score.

The announcement appeared on the front page of the *Launceston Examiner*, 2 April 1842, at that time celebrating its third week of publication. It is still the Launceston newspaper, one of the oldest in Australia. The first trees had been cleared on the site of the town only thirty-six years before, but by 1842 there was not only a good newspaper, there were already good stone-built houses, usually of one storey, and the Kavanaghs would have had little difficulty in recognising where they lived, Brisbane Street, today. In England the colonies were thought of as almost permanently rough and backward places, but contemporary prints suggest that Launceston, after little more than a generation, from scratch, was as comfortable a town as an equivalent in England, or Ireland. To speed up the building, there was of course free, convict, labour.

Being Irish, the Kavanaghs could expect a muted welcome from the settled colonists. Some of the immigrant boats of the early 1840s were said, on the island, to contain 'Romanist sweepings'. English pride of race and English class-consciousness had arrived intact in Van Diemen's Land. Modern historians like O'Farrell believe that the Irish, with their strange accents and strange religion (some not even speaking English), did much to break up the 'Englishness' of Australia in this respect, and help form the distinctive, classless, Australian character. As, it is said, the influx after the Second World War of Slav and Mediterranean people changed Melbourne from being a 'wowser' town to one in which it was pleasant to live. ('Wowser' can mean anything which represents your definition of the prim, the over-respectable, the narrow.)

Impossible to travel in 'the fine A.I. Barque ARAB, 291 tons, William Westmorland commander, open for freight or charter', but it is still possible to arrive in Launceston by sea from Melbourne, crossing the Bass Strait, and so see the island for the first time from the deck of a ship, as they did.

It is difficult to imagine what it was like travelling by sail for six months, possibly steerage, but whatever the hardships it must have been a more human process than travelling for three days by air.

Is it possible to pray in an airport? At Heathrow the Muslim cleaners do; behind screens they put down mats and prostrate themselves. On the aeroplane I read George Moore's *Esther Waters* and found the phrase 'the tender and ineffable sympathies of race and religion'. We cannot say things like that now, they sound exclusive when our duty is to understand mixture; but we can feel them, as do the cleaners at Heathrow, as I had in Ireland. I finished *Esther Waters* and re-read D. H. Lawrence's *Kangaroo*, which presented an Australia I had never seen, was about to see, in a fashion entirely convincing. 'As for *people*,' the Lawrence character in it impatiently says, 'they are the same everywhere.' Up to a point: but there are differences, sometimes so great we cannot bridge them in our minds and are nagged, fatigued, by small distresses we are hardly conscious of. For example, in an Australian aeroplane, over the sub-continent of India, it was announced that we were to be served 'a continental breakfast', as though there was only one continent, as far as breakfasts were concerned. In Bombay at three o'clock in the morning by our body-time we filed past airport curio shops whose sari'd owners stood in the doorways and did not bother to importune, knowing we would be too dazed and have no Indian money and would not want their trinkets anyway. We stared at each other, shiftily. All their lives, though they circled half the globe, Patrick and Margaret never endured such assaults of human estrangement, never moved far from 'the ineffable sympathies of race and religion'. Outside the sealed windows of the airport (we were not allowed to emerge), stacked on little hillocks next to the runways, were shanties, sunbaked, under the roaring path of the shining jets; their roofs so close together, so differently angled, they looked Cubist.

As we waited to be allowed back on the aeroplane, the first-class passengers instinctively sat at one end of the waiting hall (not speaking, with several chairs' space between them) while we milled about, with children among us, steerage.

In Singapore it was the same but more expensive, air-conditioned, carpeted, so that the muzak sounded muffled, as though something had gone wrong with our ears: a Shopping Precinct in Outer Space. There, as at Heathrow, was a multitude of Japanese insistently buying things, the same things their counterparts had bought in Heathrow.

Another such experience in Sydney and by the time freedom came, in early-morning Melbourne, stung by impressions impossible to make sense of, light-headed with sleeplessness, I dumped my bag at the ferry, which did not cross the strait to Launceston until evening, and on a Sunday morning with the promise of heat to come, I asked a cab to take me to the middle of town. He dropped me outside the famous pub, *Young and Jackson*, on what turned out to be Anzac Day.

The centre of Melbourne is reminiscent of the centre of Liverpool, seemingly of about the same period, but red instead of yellow; red glazed brick, smoke-darkened. The pub was shut, as was the rest of the town, but already slightly interested, slightly derisive groups were gathering on the pavement. After a while the motley, informal, hours-long Anzac parade began, a commemoration of the landing in Gallipoli. Each group bore lists of battle honours, from the Boer War to Vietnam, painted on twin-poled banners that young holders, sometimes girls, struggled to keep upright when the air took them and they billowed like spinnaker sails. Behind them came old veterans and young ones, medals bouncing, held on by safety pins, in uniform or not, looking martially straight ahead or talking to each other. The crowd was amused and usually silent, sometimes raising a thin cheer when they saw somebody they knew. 'Slightly interested, slightly derisive'? It began to seem that this mixture of attitudes added up to something identifiable, original, at one with the informality and tattiness of the parade itself. There were girls and young boys marching, wearing medals, presumably their fathers', there were tentative and puzzling bagpipe bands, also unisex. Some of it was reminiscent of the Boys' Brigade, though not so well drilled. But you sensed the occasion was both friendly and critical: no one was going to be allowed to play the hero, nor was anyone in that crowd going to appear moved, yet the procession went on – it was more of a procession than a parade – for miles and for hours, and the pavements stayed crowded, although the young men outside Young and Jackson's pretended they were only waiting for the pub to open, were only there for the beer – which they were and were not. Australian public feeling was a subtle business.

There was something new about it, an absence, which had been changed into an attitude. The purpose of the marchers was clear: a sweating commemoration of their own pasts and of Australia's; but the crowd exuded a feeling that, in an unconscious way, it expected to be bullied into being more orderly, into showing more respect than it felt, or in a way that did not suit it. Because they were not bullied in this way they seemed slightly lost, uncertain, and because there was no authority for them to resist their derision had no target except themselves, so it expanded into friendliness and teasing. Everything about the deliberate lack of pomp was anti-imperial, but for most of the watchers the Empire was not even a memory, or only a distant, occluded one. Nevertheless, they waited for the schoolmaster to come, so that they could cheek him; but he did not come, so they were in the process of evolving their own authority, based on a (sceptical) respect for each other. It was exciting to observe but made a stranger wonder how many more Anzac parades there could be.

At a bus-stop I fell into conversation with a thoughtful-looking man who had dropped out of the parade and, medals still pinned on the lapel of his suit, was going home. Diffident at first, not suspicious, but courteously fearful of giving offence – those few hours in Australia had already shown people more natural and polite than we are at home – he explained that a mood had grown up about Anzac Day, a sense that Australia had been used, had been required to take part in, its sons to die in, wars far distant from its own concerns; and had afterwards been abandoned by England, who then looked after herself. So the Anzac commemoration lost its way and purpose, the ethos that sustained it evaporated. This he said in so many words, but what he did not go on to say, perhaps from modesty, was that it had turned into something else, something within reasonable limits formal, joshing, sceptical yet serious: something Australian.

His bus arrived, he left me with instructions about how to find one for the ferry, but they were complicated and I decided to walk.

I wanted to walk because, from the early-morning cab, I had glimpsed some 'original Melbourne' buildings, of a kind that might have been there when the Kavanaghs passed through. They had a Wild West look, single-storeyed; they were set back from a pillared veranda, the kind on which the sheriff might sit, chair tipped back, his boot on the veranda rail. I wanted to see anything that was left of the world Patrick saw.

Under the arches of a railway was a sign, 'Museum of the Bush', and a large-eyed woman rose welcomingly when I peered in, so I had to enter a series of dark tunnels that boomed with the noise of trains passing overhead, and through these reverberations could just be heard a tape playing, of a reedy male voice singing unaccompanied songs about the Outback. She told me that she had made with her own hands the seven thousand rough clay models of sheep, sheep-shearers, sheep-shearing, that lined the sides of the seemingly endless tunnels. Each bore its label, drawing attention to times past; there was even a model of her father's dog and its kennel, with the legend, 'This one's for you, Dad!'.

On the very first morning I had stumbled upon a dispiriting parody, or perhaps an apt criticism, of the sort of search that I was setting out to make in words. The sculptor's Australian family tree was on the wall; and she even had an Irish name. She had been brought up among the Old Ways of the Outback and she lamented their passing. The thin old voice on the loudspeaker, when it could be heard between trains, also appeared to be caught between a boast of past hardship and a lament about modern Australia. The sculptor caught me at the exit and said yearningly, 'There's a free cup of tea that goes with the visit.' Panic struck, I blurted out something non-sensical, 'No! No! I have to cross the river!' and escaped from the near-dark into the bright and now deserted Sunday street.

I said it because I only knew I had to cross the river Parra, which was not far from the Wild West houses I wanted to see; I remembered no other landmark. Outside those tunnels I was at once lost. By now the pubs were opening, the parade was over, and I could go in and ask the way. But before doing that I paused, and thought – infinitely more quickly than the time it will take to describe – that the problem in Australia, in the Catholic Church, in Carlow, in me, was not only 'authority'; there was also for me the problem of 'involvement'. (Perhaps to be involved means the acceptance of some form of authority.) I could no more have become 'involved' with that woman, have noted the degrees and expressions of her amiable dottiness, than I could have stayed much longer with those clay sheep. Observation without involvement; I was a man permanently on the run.

Ivor Gurney wrote an interesting poem about this. He thought that as soon as he became involved he ceased to be a poet, whereas the people he admired, the ordinary soldiers of the First World War, could both be involved and retain their unconscious sense of poetry. He concluded, therefore, that his poetry was 'a girl's fancies', a form of nonsense, and in him it was now dead. He has a point. My consolation had to be that, after so deciding, he then wrote some of his best poems.

I went into the first pub I saw, where I knew I would never

become involved, could only observe, and felt immediately, in an unexpected way, at home.

At first there was the language difficulty, as in any foreign place. It was hot, and a long air-conditioned flight dries you out. I wanted a pint of beer, knew Australia was metric so asked for 'a glass' and was presented with something tiny. It was explained that if I wanted a bigger glass I should ask for 'a pot' but when I did so it seemed only slightly larger. Nevertheless the parade, medals and all, piling into the back bar, glimpsed through the serving hatch, had already reached a state of conviviality difficult to explain if their glasses had to be replenished after a sip. Then it became clear how it was done; they ordered by the jug, or 'juggie'. 'Another juggie, Brucie, mate!'

The 'mate' was good to hear but there, at the serving hatch, briefly appeared a sweet Gloucestershire face I knew well. Though I could not put a name to it, I could place him standing by a certain gate at home. I wondered whether I should go round and challenge him, but the coincidence was surely impossible, and what was going on behind that hatch was entirely Australian.

Anyone who has been in the British army, however briefly, and however he may dislike this, is doomed for ever unconsciously to give people military ranks on the grounds of their appearance. He learns to do so in the army in order to survive, and it sticks; perhaps it is based on haircuts. You can recognise an officer from behind. Those first-class passengers at Singapore had instinctively formed themselves into a separate Officers' Mess, and they had first-class haircuts. Behind the hatch were men who looked like brigadiers, with neat moustaches, well-fed complexions, smart wings of greying hair swept back behind their ears; there was also present every other kind of rank (I could stare because they could not see me) down to the type of the shifty orderly corporal who has managed to get himself permanently Excused Boots. But not only, chipped blue at the neck or glossily barbered, did they all drink together, there seemed no constraint or falseness of geniality among them, as there always was in a British Mess at Christmas when the ranks changed places, and officers waited on the men. The brigadier slopped beer from his jug into the glass of the barrackroom lawyer, and vice versa, with equal naturalness. Perhaps I had it wrong, and the clipped moustaches were corporals, and the Brueghel-looking figures, even the gentle, remembered Gloucestershire face, were the colonels, and did it matter anyway? What a pleasure it would be to shed that terrible English load. It seemed to have been shed in Melbourne.

The directions had again been hard to understand and once outside I was lost for the second time. I had not spoken to the Gloucestershire man. I had fled from the 'Museum of the Bush'. I still had 'a girl's fancies' and still stared, fancifully, from the mouth of my own tunnel. It was a girl, twenty-five years before, who had shown me how you could involve yourself in the world without losing yourself. It seemed I had still, without her, not learned how.

At least I could find my way back to that ferry. There was no one about, not even a car. I was now in the suburbs, and the streets were widening into used-car lots and typewriter concessionaires that were probably deserted even on weekdays. There was no way of telling even if I was walking in the right direction, towards the sea. I grew hotter and clung to the shadows. At about the moment I wondered whether I was in trouble – on the fraying edges of towns you can be afflicted by the same atavistic tremor you receive in a forest when you realise you have passed that dead tree before, and are walking in circles; here I believed I had passed that bunch of second-hand cars for the second time, they were surrounded by the same pennanted rope – at a time when I was thinking I ought to walk the dusty miles back into Melbourne and start again, a car appeared, approached and stopped. Inside it a middle-aged couple bent their heads over a street-map, and I guessed they were lost too. I stood in front of their bonnet, waved, called, but nothing would make them look up. I knocked on their window and, startled, the wife wound the window down, a little.

'Lost? So are we, the place has changed so much. The ferry? You're miles off. Jump in.' 'No, no.' 'Yes, yes.' 'Oh well, very kind.' 'When's the ferry? You've ages. Seen Melbourne? We'll show you.'

It could have happened anywhere, but this was Australia and the quick hospitality seemed Australian. They showed me Betjemanesque clapboard and wrought-iron suburbs – Williams Town, St Kilda's – originally fishermen's houses, or the houses of whalers, now expensively done up, but they must always have been beautiful. Their own house was across the bay; would I come there? I was too tired so we went to a pub called the Old Vic and they were relieved, for the visitor's sake, that so much of the old furnishing and plaster had been preserved.

On the way to the ferry, in a park, we came upon a lively scene, unexpected on that now deserted day: picnickers and kite-flyers and gambolling children, all gathered together among their parked cars. 'New Australians! Must be!' snorted the husband, and his wife turned from the wheel and winked in my direction. Later I was to be told that it was these who had improved Melbourne beyond recognition. A traveller is at the mercy of what he is told, but at least I had learned that old Australians recognised a category called 'new' ones, not always with pleasure; that picturesque small houses for working men have now become chic middle-class properties; that changes, and the resentments they bring, always seem to be the same everywhere.

The *Abel Tasman* – even its name a celebration of the pre-imperial, indeed, pre-Euro-Australian past – loomed up white and big and welcoming. There had been talk of my guides' grown-up children and I asked what these did: one was a sculptor, one an art teacher, another a community worker.

Their mother recited this with pride while their father, with certain facial movements, nasal expulsions of air, suggested that his pride was mixed with a doubtfulness about the utility of these occupations. Searching for an adjective that would please both I said that they sounded – interesting. It pleased. 'They *are* interesting,' said their mother, gratefully (the father twitching, playing a tune through his nostrils), 'they're not only concerned about *money!*' So that was what most young Australians were only concerned about? It sounded like home.

5

Van Diemen's Land

'There's Tassie!' came the cry on the deck at dawn. 'I'm not an Australian, I'm a Taswegian!' announced the woman proudly.

We had crossed the often dreaded Bass Strait smoothly, during a calm night, and had no sight of the islands where the first white sealers lived, with their captive Tasmanian women, or of Flinders Island, where George Augustus Robinson had settled the last Tasmanians at Wybalenna, which means 'Black Man's Home', to keep them safe from the sealers. Robinson was a Methodist, from London, who learned the aboriginal language and wanted to make Christians of them, but the few that were left pined away on Flinders Island and died.

The Bass Strait only filled with water, separating Tasmania from mainland Australia, ten, perhaps twenty thousand years ago, and during that time the Tasmanians were cut off from the rest of the world. They developed less than the aborigines of the mainland; they seem to have had no spear-throwers, boomerangs, shields. Then came the sealers, the whalers, the escaped convicts, who killed the men and turned the women into slaves. Parts of Tasmania became a bandit society, and the natives were slaughtered for sport. By 1828 they knew enough to set fire to white farms, and enough English to swear, 'Go away you white buggers! What business have you here?' (or so a burnt-out farmer reported at the time). Lloyd Robinson crisply and bitterly sums up their fate in *A History of Tasmania*: 'Having moved during a period of 27 years from innocence and curiosity to bewilderment to annoyance to fury to fear to frenzy, they were mopped up by the victorious Europeans.'

In 1830 Governor Arthur made an attempt to round up the remnants of them, a line of beaters fanning out across the island. Again, this was supposed to be for their protection, to put them on the Flinders Island settlement; but not many were found, there were probably not many left – and those that were found soon died of white men's diseases – also, it seems, from sadness, within sight of the main island.

I had wondered for years whether Patrick had been one of the party of beaters, and it was good to learn that he could not have been, in 1830. In 1842, his arrival year, a surviving group of aboriginals was found, a man and wife and four children, who escaped. They were probably the last of the original people of Van Diemen's Land. In Robinson's establishment the last man died in 1869 and the last woman in 1876. That was that.

Did any memory of the first Tasmanians' fate poison the air of the island when Patrick arrived, or poison it now, and memories of the punishments given to convicts?

'There's Tassie!' was a glad cry (to rhyme with 'jazzy'): the Australians were fond of abbreviations. The woman next to me was called 'Marj'; a little plaque announced this, pinned to her bosom. She was being teased about her absent husband, Doug.

I watched the approaching coastline, the first descendant of Patrick, from the Old World, to do so for a hundred and fifty years. Did he stand with his child in his arms, his wife at his elbow, like some kind of reversal of Ford Madox Brown's *The Last of England*? If he did he must have felt the same astonishment, or greater; I had flown for thirty-six hours and sailed for twelve but he had floated uncomfortably for six months across the known world to the furthest corner of it and what he saw was what I saw – the hills of Carlow.

There may have been more trees on the shoreline then, the slow green slope up from the sea may not yet have become pasture, as now it is, but the shape of the land was as gentle and welcoming, and in the distance were blue, not at all threatening, hills. What he felt would have depended on how much he had in his pocket and who, if anyone, was waiting to meet him. But he was arriving at what looked like the familiar, another Ireland at the bottom of the world.

A bird on a post that stuck out of the sea was, I discovered, a white-faced shag, a kind of bird I had not seen before, and I welcomed its strangeness, because it switched me into a wider, non-human world, as I stood next to Marj and heard talk about Doug and about Tassie. We try to make the world less frightening by patronising it, and cosy abbreviations are one way of doing so. The wild white-faced shag, which the old Tasmanians would have known, was a reminder that we can never quite succeed. The temptation to suburbanise Australia spiritually must have been irresistible, it is so vast and empty, the countries the settlers came from so frighteningly far away. The cosy layers of the familiar under which we try to bury our fear would by now be thick in Van Diemen's Land. It would not be easy to dig through to Patrick's island.

He and Margaret and Mary Ann would have sailed down the river Tamar to Launceston (one of the first governors of the island came from Cornwall, and he too wanted to feel at home), but now the river is silted, the boat too big, so we disembarked at Devonport on the coast and waited for the coach. The little waiting room, hung with the kind of faded photographs of beauty spots that used to decorate English railway carriages, reminded me of childhood, and there was an air of old-fashioned middle-aged competence and calm about it; a good place in which to scribble notes. So I wrote, 'Interest in past = interest in supernatural – future.' I no longer know exactly what that meant, except that to think about the past you have to engage with departed spirits. 'Present fine, Marj's badge and jokes about Doug, but past and future needed, to give it significance.' I might have added that the white-faced shag was needed too.

A fair-haired American girl sat next to me thumbing through tourist leaflets about water-skiing resorts and wild life parks ('Meet the Tasmanian Devils!') and a glimpse of these depressed me, because I did not want Tasmania now to be like everywhere else. She said to me, 'Isn't it thrilling?', and I said I didn't know yet, which puzzled her, and was priggish. 'Then why have you come?' she said. Her reasoning was simple: she was on holiday, therefore where she had come to was thrilling, or she had wasted her money. The difference between us was that I was older.

Besides, my answer had not been true. I had been thrilled on the deck, in fine autumn weather, an unknown yet familiar-looking island approaching. I had not been on my own for so long a time for years, and had felt trepidation, also, for I was about to try to take in a continent, alone. A body of my age has developed various bugs, physical and mental; perhaps I had left the journey too late. But I was in my favourite position, relished since childhood, looking out from the mouth of the tunnel, nothing required of me except to look and listen.

We boarded the bus and it was clear, as always, how difficult we make those simple activities. I wanted to look at Tasmania, listen to it, maybe we all did, but on the bus it was insisted that we look at over-coloured video-film, set dead-centre in the bus's internal forehead and aimed directly at our pineal glands: a British film about pirates, most of whom wore black eyepatches and all of whom swigged rum and said 'Yo ho ho'.

'Do we have to have that rubbish in our ears?' said an Australian voice behind me to his companion. Did we? It almost deprived me of the power to see or hear anything else.

When the driver came round to collect our tickets I asked him if it would be possible to turn it off, conscious of my tweed, my age, my English voice. He was startled (and no support came from the complaining Australian behind).

'There've been people on the bus before, it's half-way through, they'll want to see how it ends. *I* don't want it,' he muttered, in a different voice. 'I have to put up with it three times a week.'

He returned to his seat, switched on his engine, and took hold of his microphone: 'I've had complaints about the video!' (I liked the inaccurate plural.) 'Sorry.' Then his voice fell, he began to mutter again, almost to himself, 'I can't *stand* complaints!', let in the clutch *and turned the video off*.

I have had no success with that sort of complaint anywhere else, ever. I listened for disappointed murmurs, prepared to give way, but none came.

I suspected he turned it off because he was sick of it himself; but I had reason to ponder that event throughout my time in Tasmania. In a form that seemed to connect with it, I came across a similar reaction, which appeared to have something to do with authority, or a memory of it. When I asked someone the way, for example, two times out of three they seemed to have to rouse themselves from some sort of half-sleep. They would stare and then, as though dragging their consciousness like a huge and unwieldy fish to the surface, became aware and helpful. This happened so often I wondered if Australians were stunned by the spaces around them, their attentions diffused, so that they had to draw themselves together when confronted by an unexpected question.

For a long time, as I noticed this, I tried to remember what it reminded me of. Then I remembered, and wished I had not, because it suggests a class condescension I do not believe I possess. It is another memory of National Service in the army. Sometimes, as a very junior officer, you have to approach someone below you in rank (there is no other way of putting that) who is off-duty and on his own territory. He may be lolling in unbuttoned ease, in his own mess-hall. (It was always surprising how extravagantly private soldiers were able to relax, in terms of disordered clothes and physical position and fug. It was not like that among us boarding-school boys, we had early been inhibited from the natural.) He would look up in a blurred fashion, it would dawn on him that he was being addressed by an *officer*, he would straighten up, a little (if he did so too much or too quickly the mickey was about to be taken), you would say, 'No, no, I only want to know where Private So-and-So is', and he would take his feet off the table and be helpful, if you were lucky. That is how it was, and that, precisely, is what the Tasmanian response reminded me of.

Much later I discussed this with the Tasmanian-born novelist C. J. Koch, wondering if I had imagined it. Perhaps he teased but he seemed to think not, and laughed: 'We still respond to the voice of the Redcoat!' Or the tweed-coat. Did I really give that impression, and were those things still in the Tasmanian consciousness? Both were possible, alas.

Meanwhile, outside the bus, video-free Tasmania unfolded. If the island looked like Carlow from the sea the landscape now was like parts of the Sussex Downs, grazed by stone-colour, kangaroo-colour sheep. I kept thinking for a moment that these were kangaroos, partly because of the colour but also because, out of some extra-Darwinian sympathy with those native animals, Tasmanian sheep seem to have developed longer back legs, which prop them permanently in the grazing position.

From those first moments of looking at it, Tasmania struck me as a place like other places but significantly unlike them as well. It reminded you of them and it did not; it was a place of its own and therefore did not feel remote because it posed the question: remote from what?

Peter Conrad, another Tasmanian-born writer, confesses in his book about his return to the island, *Down Home*, that he once burst into unexplained tears as a child, and this, he now believes, was because he had a sense of being cut off from the importances of the outside world. Tasmania, he suggests, is an offshore island, off the shore of another offshore island, Australia, which to some extent disowns it (from the map of Australia on some tourist ashtrays Tasmania is left off altogether), and has therefore been forced to push itself spiritually over the South Pole and begin the slow journey northwards, to England. To this he ascribes 'the Englishness' of Tasmania.

I can only say, as a visitor from England, that I did not notice this Englishness. Nor is it clear what being 'cut off' in that sense means. It suggests there is somewhere to be cut off from, as the early Tasmanians were from Australia. But in this case what is meant: London? New York? Oxford? It was important to consider this, because it affected Patrick. Did he, and others like him, feel 'cut off' from Carlow? He never went back there. Perhaps he could not afford to, but in the journeys that followed I formed the impression that the world he found and the world he made, in Van Diemen's Land and then in New Zealand, would be roughly the equivalent of any he could have found 'at home', and almost certainly preferable. To some extent he would bring 'home' with him, in the sense of race, nationality, religion – the last powerfully reinforcing the other two. It is writers and artists and academics who invent the myth of distance, the snobbery of the 'centre'. In order to prove to themselves that they have arrived they invent a destination. Most people do not feel 'cut off'; there is only life itself, and that can be lived as well – better, for many – in Tasmania as anywhere else.

At the hotel in Brisbane Street, chosen because the Kavanaghs had lived in the street, the manager was a young Indian from Bombay, who had come to Launceston as a child, one of six. Soon after they arrived his father had died, and their mother worked to bring them up. It was hard. Was it worth it? He closed his eyes. 'Oh yes! I would be nowhere else!'

The pub opposite the hotel was called The Royal Oak, (the noise from which, on a Saturday night, made the Indian hotel

Brisbane Street, Launceston c. 1840

manager wince). In the 'mini-bar' of the bedroom was every kind of drink known in England, biscuits and sweets in familiar wrappings with familiar names. On the bedside telephone to England our voices echoed, bouncing off the satellite, and we stopped, so as not to interrupt what was only an echo of our own last words. Was Tasmania only a muffled echo of England's last words, bouncing off that distant northern island? It did not seem so. I regretted answering that American girl as I had. There *was* something thrilling about the place. Not least because its landscape must have appeared so familiar to Patrick.

6

Launceston

In *Kangaroo*, the D. H. Lawrence character, Richard, is tempted towards revolutionary politics by the man nicknamed 'Kangaroo' because his ideas of revolution, based on brotherly love, attract Richard; but something holds him back.

'You see,' stammered Richard, 'it needs more than a belief of men in each other.'

'But what else is there to believe in? Quacks? Medicine men? Scientists and politicians?'

'It *does* need some sort of religion.'

'Well then – well then – the religious question is ticklish, especially here in Australia. But all the churches are founded on Christ. And Christ says Love one another.'

Richard laughed suddenly.

'That makes Christ into another political agent,' he said.

'Well then – I'm not deep enough for these matters. But surely you know how to square it with religion. Seems to me it *is* religion – love one another.'

'Without a God.'

'Well – as I say – it's Christ's teaching, and that ought to be God enough.'

Richard was silent, his heart heavy.

He goes out and does ordinary things, visits the post office to buy some stamps, looks along the busy street, on impulse he hails a friend – and 'suddenly the whole thing switched away from him: "Jaz," he said, "I want to drive round the Botanical Gardens and round the spit there – and I want to look at the peacocks and the cockatoos." '

Sitting in the public gardens of Launceston, I thought, this could be described as his 'white-faced shag moment'. Such widenings of perspective are like a momentary unclenching of the soul, and are important. On my first full morning in Launceston I sat in the gardens and watched the monkeys.

They did not cheer me as the emus and cockatoos and peacocks of Sydney had cheered Richard/D.H. Lawrence. They seemed desolate on their rock with a moat full of soiled water round them. One stood in the moat, looking up for titbits from a group of laughing children, the water giving him a clinging set of bathing-drawers, turning his grey fur black. Monkeys are supposed not to have dignity, but all animals do, given a chance, and there was an uncomfortable pathos in that one, standing in water to beg for food. They were inappropriate in that trim little Victorian park, with its wrought-iron bandstand and its unexplained Russian cannon on a plinth. I later asked someone why the monkeys were there. He shrugged and said, 'They always have been', as though they were found in their cement and moated isolation when the park was first enclosed. Nor could anyone satisfactorily explain the presence of the cannon. Perhaps Tasmanians are as little interested in their past as most people are everywhere. Much of their past, though brief, is perhaps best not thought about at all.

Peter Conrad gives a brief account of his native island:

Tasmania, despite its short life, is a palimpsest of different, antagonistic cultures. It was owned at first by the aborigines, who understood it and indexed it. They assigned a spirit to every mountain, stream and cave, deriving their ancestry from the land. They were dis-possessed when the place became a penal outpost of England. A terrain their legends had placated turned ugly overnight. The topography of Van Diemen's Land was an illustration of hell, a catalogue of moral alarms – the dentated chasms of the Tasman Peninsula, the black gulf of Macquarie Harbour, the unnutritious forests which made escaped convicts into cannibals. When transportation ended, the state changed its name and (so it hoped) its identity. Now it is a genteel community of graziers who settled the midlands in mansions of what might be crumbly Cotswold stone. Since then, overlaid on their pastoral regime, industry has arrived to torment the land, rather than patiently tending it like the good shepherd: the mines of the west coast, the reservoirs and power-stations of the highlands.

Of course it is true. (Macquarie Harbour and the Tasman Peninsula were the sites of two of the harshest, second-punishment, penal settlements.) The story of Tasmania's first fifty years is hard to contemplate, because of genocide, because of European brutalities to each other.

But no visitor can see a place through the eyes of someone born there, through the bewilderments of childhood, frustrations of adolescence; it was not there that he suffered them.

What was striking me now as I sat in the park, despite the past that had surrounded it, was what an obviously pleasant place Launceston had become – apart from the old-lag monkeys. Would not such a place, newly founded, aspire to the 'genteel', as the sparks fly upward, above all in a society that was initially a penal settlement? Also, industry always 'torments' the earth, everywhere.

Thinking this, sitting on a park bench, I became aware of the extraordinary industry of a man raking up leaves. The man never looked up, never paused in his tireless raking. It was nine-thirty in the morning and already he had pulled together dozens of cone-shaped piles; he worked as though his life depended on it, or – such thoughts come unbidden in

Tasmania, and perhaps they should – as though an unseen overseer stood near, fingering a lash. It was probably such industry that had built the town so quickly. The first clearance of the site, in 1806, had taken place near where I sat, near Tamar Street. The soldier who had been in charge of the clearing party (John Dell, from Reading) lived in the town until he was a hundred and three, in Brisbane Street. He died in 1866, an inescapable 'character' buttonholing everybody with his tales. Patrick must have known him: he had twenty-five years in which to do so, in an increasingly elegant little town; he must often have talked to the man who supervised the felling of the first tree.

The age of some of the houses is astonishing; they must have been built almost at once. They are usually of one storey, wood or yellow sandstone, set back behind a pillared veranda decorated with curlicues of wrought iron. They are delicate and pretty and often larger than they seem, because if the land falls away behind them a second storey can be added underneath. Their Australian democracy ('No Upstairs/ Downstairs about us, mate') can therefore be deceptive, and the houses on one side of a street can be larger than those on the other, though each side looks the same. There are newer houses and shops, mostly mid- or late-Victorian, with some 1930s art deco shops in between, but the place has a homogeneous country-town air, with hills either side of it, hills behind, and the river in front.

At the theatre in Brisbane Street that morning June Bronhill was giving a concert of old musical-comedy favourites, and the street was filled with Sunset Home minibuses from which elderly people were being helped or wheeled, come to singalong with her. There was no temptation to think 'how like England of thirty years ago'; it was not like England. The children coming out of school at lunchtime, neat in their blazers, had no temptation to disorder their clothes, as they would have in England: ties still accurately knotted, socks neatly pulled up (perhaps daunting in their lack of rebelliousness), with a gloss on their skins and a light in their mostly fair hair that made them look as though they belonged to a new race altogether. Had the mad experiment of transportation worked after all? The insane rationalism of the Enlightenment, which believed, or affected to believe, that if you expelled your 'criminal class' – those you did not hang – you would thereby genetically improve your own stock, had been proved nonsense at home. What of these fourth-generation descendants (many of them) of convicts over whom John Mitchel, Irish revolutionist, had grimly mused in the 1850s, deciding that perhaps four or five generations hence they might result in something 'almost human'? (He would have hanged them all). Whether they were human or not, in any significant way, it was too early to tell, as with all children; but physically they were superb.

This is Launceston in the 1980s; what was it like in the 1840s? There was an exhibition of early colonial Tasmanian painting in the Victoria Museum and I went there hoping for townscapes; but in the main it was only 'views', suspiciously British-looking, as though the painters were more concerned with what would be acceptable to their patrons than with what was in front of their eyes – if they could see it at all, because to 'see' the unfamiliar takes time.

The exhibition, I learned, was a great event in Tasmania, the first occasion those paintings had been gathered together; until then few had realised that Tasmania had any tradition of painting at all. It did something for Tasmanian pride, helped to salve the island's sense of inferiority, of being nowhere, at the edge of the world.

Such feelings are difficult for a visitor to take account of; he cannot know how many snubs and condescensions, real or imagined, the place has received. Yet no country has been more snubbed and derided than Ireland, and there I get no sense of this provincialism. Perhaps there the international nature of Roman Catholicism has helped. (Maybe it was England that turned herself into a province, out of the European mainstream, which is why she had to build an empire.) What I wanted to find out, because of Patrick and others, was not the extent to which Tasmania was or was not an imitation of 'the mother country' but what the early settlers made of the place and of themselves when they got there.

You only had to go downstairs into the museum below to be reminded that Tasmania, Van Diemen's Land, had a unique problem of identity. From 1803 to 1853 it received not only 'Romanist sweepings' but the sweepings, Romanist or otherwise, of every gaol in Britain. Locally these were talked about in semi-heroic terms; one had stolen a handkerchief, or been falsely accused of doing so, had been transported and then treated with vile cruelty by his or her oppressors. Some of this is sometimes true, but most of those transported were second or third offenders against property, and although, in E. P. Thompson's fine phrase 'the worst offence against property was to have none', they were not always, and not often, blushing innocents.

The need to make them appear so is understandable. In the museum is a 'punishment' fork: an ordinary garden fork with the tines made unnecessarily thick, inlaid with lead, so that it must have been nearly impossible to use. This horrible object is a minor indication of the stupid meanness of punishment that attended a second offence. For those mad enough or brave enough to continue to defy, the punishments spiralled into nightmare, dutifully noted in copperplate: every lash, every day in irons, every week in darkness and silence, and of course every lonely, ignominious death as a result of punishment. The early free citizens would have had to cultivate a tactical blindness to what was going on around them. As for the convicts, most of them must have been cowed, because if they kept their heads down and behaved they were given free pardons reasonably quickly (the government did not want to have to pay for them). It was tempting to see an outcome of this in the strange, startled politeness, in the obedience of pedestrians to the 'Don't Walk' signs at intersections: these only changed when all four streams of traffic were halted and this often took a long time, but even with no cars in sight few crossed until the light changed to 'Walk'.

Near the 'punishment' fork, the balls and chains, and the convict uniforms, the museum kept a library of rare books, and in response to my pestering I was led to a book written by one settler who came out as a boy from Suffolk in 1838 to join his parents; not much could have changed by the time Patrick arrived.

> In one of our rambles in the town we met a chain gang –a number of convicts, perhaps forty or fifty, dressed in coarse cloth of black and yellow, and each wearing a small peaked leather cap. They marched in a line two abreast, every man having a chain about three feet long attached to his legs just above the ankle, and suspended in the middle by a small strap to a belt around his body; and along the centre of the line ran another chain to which each man was secured, and thus all were fastened together. These men were going to work under the control of a warder armed with a musket. That was my introduction to a convict settlement, and young as I was the sight produced in me a feeling of revulsion, and I was greatly shocked.

That is by Henry Button, who became editor of the *Launceston Examiner* and one of the leaders of the fight against transportation. In his book, *Flotsam and Jetsam*, there are tales of blackened bodies hanging in gibbets, but perhaps these would not be surprising to Patrick, from Carlow.

Maybe Launceston did not develop as quickly as, for Patrick's sake, I had hoped. Button arrives from England four years before Patrick: 'But how shall I describe the shock I received on reaching home? *Home*! a miserable little four-roomed wooden cottage in Bathurst Street, still standing. Was it for this I had left the comforts and elegance of the large house in Ipswich, and sailed sixteen thousand miles across the ocean? Where was the three-storey house I had been told my father had built, and which I had been eager to see?' Not having known his parents since he was an infant he did not recognise them, and his father 'introduced us to a meanly clad and fragile-looking woman whom he spoke of as "our mother". It was too much for me: the strain and disappointment was too acute, and I burst into tears.'

Sad for both; but his account of early Launceston, of schools being built, churches and schools founded, is like the background story to an American western, a natural attempt to create the genteel out of whatever came to hand, but a western set in a prison. Most of the servants were convicts, and these are regarded with a mixture of amusement and fear (as were servants, doubtless, in England). A cook, too often interrupted, declares, 'she wouldn't have any mistress traipsing into her kitchen, *and she had been sent out here for killing a man*.' (This is a convict using the power of the unknown over her employers: if that had been her crime she would not have got as far as Van Diemen's Land.) In Button's book you sense an emergent middle class defining itself, amusing each other with stories about a lower class which was officially defined and controlled. There is unease, because of the special nature of the class: 'Most of the men employed about the establishment, and indeed generally then, were prisoners and lived on the premises. On Sundays, therefore, it was deemed prudent that at least one of the family should stay at home during the hours of the divine service, to see that everything was correct.' Button was a Congregationalist, and he says nothing about the servants going to divine service. Perhaps they were Irish (many were) and therefore Roman Catholic. Throughout his long life in Launceston Button mentions no friend who has an Irish name.

As in a Western there were Bad Men, 'bushrangers', escaped convicts. There are many tales of break-ins, murders and consequent hangings. But there was no sheriff, no Wyatt Earp to clean up the township. The inhabitants had to look after themselves and seem to have been good at it. It was not only bushrangers they had to fear; there were the soldiers themselves, whose conditions were not much better than those of the prisoners, and in terms of punishment sometimes worse. (When John Mitchel was imprisoned in Bermuda he was told that a fifth of the convicts there were former soldier-guards who had changed their status on purpose, by deserting.)

But the settlers seemed equal even to these. Forty or fifty men of the 96th Regiment 'attacked several public houses and private dwellings, smashing windows, doors, and everything that came their way; one of the inmates was badly assaulted. They were checked by the occupier of one inn, who defended his property with a brace of pistols, one of which he fired at the mob, slightly wounding one soldier. A repetition on the following night was threatened, but fortunately did not come off, as a number of citizens well armed were prepared to deal with the rioters.' It really was like the Wild West; this was in 1845, when Patrick would be just about settled in, with his young family. In 1853 'the discontinuance of transportation rendered the presence of Imperial troops no longer necessary, and they were gradually but entirely withdrawn', which must have been a relief. They still had convicts there, but in August of that year: 'An address to Queen Victoria was adopted expressing gratitude and joy at the abandonment of convict traffic to the island. And as a declaration of their joy, the huge and bulky gallows was dismantled brick by brick.'

The town must have been improving all the time; by 1860, when they first switched on the gas lamps in the streets, the population had risen to 10,000. Nevertheless, in all the accounts I could find there were no traces so far of Patrick and his world. The only Kavanagh mentioned was a member of Martin Cash's famous gang of bushrangers, and for a moment I entertained an unlikely hope; but he was hanged, poor man – he was not Patrick. There was nothing for it but to burrow in the local history archives.

I had expected these to be quiet places, haunted by the occasional vague scholar who might be persuaded to help the amateur investigator. As soon as the door was opened you saw that inside was a kind of bedlam. They overflowed with eager genealogists.

There were tall, leather-bound volumes of registers and newspapers round the walls and these were being pulled from the shelves greedily, their pages turned frenziedly – not turned at all, those yellowed pages, brittle as dead leaves, but crumpled impatiently over and away with the edge of the hand, or with all four fingers. Fortunately for its survival, most of the material was on microfilm, and there was a battery of microfiche machines, into which the film was fed and appeared on a screen, which could be rolled or stopped for closer examination and note-taking, by pressing certain buttons. Each of these machines was surrounded by waiting groups with the frustrated air of people standing outside a too-long-occupied telephone booth, while the lucky person using it punched the buttons like a fruit-machine gambler in Las Vagas. 'Got him!' one of them cried, nose against the screen, 'I *knew* he was there! He was a Rogers!' A pleasant-faced woman nearby was quietly cursing as she apparently unseeingly riffled the pages of the register, too quickly for her to be able to read it, as though she had gone mad. She confessed that she had: 'It becomes an obsession. You wake up at two-thirty in the morning and think: Was there something I missed today? These bloody convicts,' she muttered, returning to her page-riffling, 'you can even learn what they *looked* like. My people were free but I can't find out a thing about them!'

The archive-haunters turned eyes glazed with screen-watching on the new, hesitant presence (briefly I had considered running away) and eventually they sat me down in front of one of the machines and taught me how to use it; they were inviting me to join their coven. (It has to be said that they were mostly middle-aged women, but that was natural; their children now gone from home, they had time to try to find out who those children's ancestors were, who they were themselves.) What had seemed like a mildly original idea in England, the exploration of roots, as it were, in reverse, not in the home country but in the colony – a friend had suggested that I call my account of it *O'Roots* – had in Australia, in its bicentennial year, become a national mania.

They told me I must run through a film of the electoral roll if he had become a householder. I knew that he had been one because I had been warned (wisely) to do as much research as I could before leaving England. But there was no Patrick Kavanagh on the electoral roll: not under K, not under C, not under 'Cavanaugh' or 'Caverner' (as in America, immigrants were at the mercy of the way clerks spelled their names); not under anything.

I suppose it took the best part of a beautiful day (outside) to discover that nothing; by which time I understood the wildness in the eyes around me. I also began to feel that Patrick wanted to elude me, just as he had eluded me and everybody else in Ireland. Perhaps he should be allowed to. My father certainly was elusive. Maybe it ran in the family.

Did the man come here at all? Or perhaps he really had taken to the bush, with fellow Irishman Martin Cash? No, there he was on the shipping-list of the *Arab*, aged twenty-three (born therefore in 1819), with his wife Margaret and his two-year-old daughter Mary Ann. He put down his trade as 'groom' and he was a bounty passenger: his fare, or part of it, paid by 'Henry Dowling'.

Here at last seemed a clue. The family tradition, originating in New Zealand (I never heard it from my father), was that Patrick had gone to the island to manage an estate for a relative. No mention of his being a groom in that tale. Perhaps it is natural to make your roots more socially glamorous than they are, more 'genteel'. But who was Henry Dowling, that he should help Patrick with his fare? He has a large entry in the Australian *Dictionary of National Biography*, which says he was sent to England by the Protestant islanders to recruit and inspect new immigrants for Van Diemen's Land. For whom he recruited these it was essential to find out, to gain any clear picture of Patrick's first days and years on the island. In other words, who, if anyone, was there to meet him?

This I failed to discover. I found professional help with the archives but in this respect they failed too. He and his family arrive, and then for many years disappear from the record.

So I was left with that *Last of England* tableau again, the man hollow-cheeked, the young woman clutching her child, having made the long journey from Carlow to queue in London in front of prosperous Henry Dowling, who looks them over, perhaps even prods them a bit, and decides they will do, as workers for some free settler he has in mind.

It may not have been like that at all, but it was strange to discover, among the mass of documentation that remains of the period, so little record of what happened to free settlers. To investigate the convicts is easy, which is why my friend in the archives was cursing.

But is it likely that Henry Dowling would encourage a Roman Catholic Irish family to come to Van Diemen's Land? There was a great local prejudice against such people. The answer was, he did not. In 1851 Patrick filled up a census form. These should have been destroyed, but they turned up this century; bundles of them were found in old chaff sacks,

Patrick's among them. By this time he is living in a house made of wood, on Brisbane Street, confesses to no trade at all and by a tick in the appropriate box states he is Church of Ireland, which is to say, Protestant.

I had been led to believe that the Kavanaghs had been Catholic through penal times and onward. In a way it pointed back to a connection with Borris, for the Kavanaghs there had become Protestant at the end of the eighteenth century.

But he had married Margaret in the Roman Catholic cathedral in Carlow, that was sure. All his children were baptised Catholics, Mary Ann in Carlow, and the rest in Launceston. Except, that is, my grandfather, Henry Paul, born around 1843/4, of whose birth no record exists.

When I discovered there was no trace of the birth of either great-grandfather or grandfather, I began to believe that they were both trying to warn me off. I finally confirmed that there is no record of Henry Paul's birth or baptism, or that of his older brother, in the archive in Hobart, and could hardly believe it. Geoffrey Stillwell, the best genealogical historian in Tasmania, was standing behind me at the time, helping, peering over my shoulder at the screen. He could not believe it either. 'Dean Butler was a careful priest!' he said.

That was the clue, I discovered by chance later. (I learned how you could become obsessed, in baffled pursuit of a not very interesting but fundamental fact.) I picked up the news sheet of the Catholic cathedral in Hobart. On the back was a history of the Catholic church in Launceston. There was no church, no Father Butler, until 1845, and my grandfather was born before that, when no records were kept. The account reveals the extent of the official dislike of Catholics at the time. Priests were at first not paid; the official rule was that 'salaries are confined to ministers whose churches have been erected for their congregation.' If you could not afford to build a church, as the Irish Catholics at first could not, you could have no priest. This was a situation that Cardinal Cullen, Margaret's uncle, sought to change, and did. Indirectly, he was to play a significant part in the story of Patrick and Margaret.

The earliest colonists, to a large extent, lapsed into near-paganism, but no worse than that to be found in the British cities of the industrial revolution. The Reverend Thomas Guthrie in 1850s Edinburgh said that he might as well have been bringing news of Christ 'on the banks of the Ganges', for all that the people he moved among knew of Christianity. The different Christian churches in Australia moved quickly to remedy this, and there was much sectarian in-fighting and pettiness. One of the dangers – and just about the only delight – of research is that you keep being side-tracked. I remember one example of this pettiness only because of the glorious name of the Church of England clergyman involved: the Reverend Vicesimus Lush. He reported that when trying to raise funds for a church he was told by a well-to-do-family that he could expect £50 if he built it near where they lived, £1 if not.

Names were always a great distraction. On the front page of the *Launceston Examiner* that reported the arrival of the *Arab* there was an account of a temperance meeting. The society was addressed 'with some vigour' on the subject of the evils of drink, by a blacksmith called Mr Tongs.

There were other names on that front page, more germane. There were lists of convicts recently absconded and still at large, their names and heights:

Beaumon	5.11
Higgins	5.5
Abbott	4.9½
Childs	5.7
MacKay	5.2
Johnson	5.
Taylor	4.11
Hogan	5.5

Those dangerous criminals chained together, for their punishment and the public safety, those endurers of the lash, users of the 'punishment' fork, those wild and savage men who took to the bush and terrorised the towns – some of them were not five feet high, the stunted, starved products of the industrial towns. These were the men Patrick and Margaret and Mary Ann had to fear, roaming near Launceston during their first week there; poor Abbot, four foot nine and a half.

Did the Kavanaghs come out with friends from Carlow? No, the list of people on the *Arab* consists mostly of English names. Perhaps they made friends with their shipmates? Perhaps they did, but after 1845, when the godparents are named at the Kavanagh christenings, the names are all Irish.

Margaret, a Catholic, clearly had her way with the religious denomination of her children; as is recorded to be the case in most mixed marriages of that time, the children were baptised in the faith of the mother. The odd thing was that the man who came out most strongly against mixed marriages was her uncle, Cullen, and the family legend was that he married her in Carlow. Did Patrick pretend to be Church of Ireland for the social advantage of it? Impossible, said one historian-priest. (Another historian-priest, in New Zealand, when he was asked the same question, said, 'What Irishman ever took seriously what he put on a piece of government paper?') But there was not much objection to mixed marriages until Cullen got going, fearful of what might happen to the grip of the church in Australia if things became too lax. It was because of him, in the 1950s, when I married my late wife Sally, that she had to take 'instruction', to her indignation, and we had to be married at a side-altar, not at the main one. None of this mattered, but it was now, thirty years later, that I learned who had started all this, a kinsman.

I was intrigued at the thought of Patrick being a groom, because he never mentions it again on official forms and claims to be all sorts of things – baker, cabinet maker, usually the trade of the previous occupier of his home – or nothing at all. When I had archival help I was told to ask for C508/60/137. That was all the information I had about the document and it sounded formidable. It had to be brought from a back room, in Hobart. There is no general access to the archives there. Too many people, it seems, had been removing the convict records of their own ancestry, or looking up those of others who would have preferred it not known. Whether you are brought something or not is at the discretion of the archivist; a disturbing thought.

On this occasion the document arrived and it turned out to be a carefully compiled list of the trades of all who left England in 1841 and arrived in Van Diemen's Land in 1842. Every conceivable trade and calling is listed, because it was a matter of great significance in a young society to discover what skills it had imported and what it still lacked. Among them is the trade of groom, which Patrick had put down on the shipping-list of the *Arab*. No groom, in that document, left England in 1841, or arrived in Van Diemen's Land in 1842.

By 1866 this apparently tradeless man, or Jack of them all, had acquired a freehold of two houses in Brisbane Street and lived in a third. He rented out these two houses and had therefore become a landlord, a species most Irishmen went to Australia to avoid. How he managed this comparative affluence (if such it was), arriving with nothing (if he did), there was no piece of paper to be found that afforded a clue.

7

The Bush

Overheard in Launceston archives: 'The ones in Hobart are quieter.' 'Yes, but it's so expensive going there.' 'I've found a nice little B and B just near them. I use it every time.' So, their search was rigorous, they went from archive to archive, finding a place to sleep nearby. Perhaps in this way a cairn of Tasmanian – of Australian – history is being erected, and one day everybody would know where they came from and who they were connected to. This was good to think about, because the uprooting had been brutal.

'To bring men and women to this Colony in such a manner is like murdering them,' said Governor Phillip, on the arrival of the Second Fleet at Sydney in 1790. The colony's Anglican chaplain, the Reverend Richard Johnson, went on board the *Surprise*, not the worst of the convict transports, and wrote to his sister: 'the landing of these people was truly affecting and shocking, great numbers were not able to walk, nor to move hand or foot. Such were slung over the ship's side in the same manner as they would sling a cask or a box, or anything of that nature. Upon their being brought up to the open air, some fainted, some died upon deck, and others in the boat before they reached the shore.'

It is some of these people that some of the women in the archives are trying to trace. Their effort is analogous to the long work after the First World War of reburying the dead in the orchard-like orderliness of the little war cemeteries scattered over northern France. These are 'genteel', if you like, but it is

precisely that quality which wrenches the heart. Past bar-
barities cannot be cured, but we can try to atone. One hundred
and fifty thousand convicts came to Australia, half of them to
Van Diemen's Land, which is about the size of Ireland, with
large areas of it uninhabitable wilderness, 'the bush'.

It was the suggested quietness of the Hobart archives that
had caught my attention in the overheard conversation.
Perhaps there I would be able to pounce, like Sherlock Holmes,
on a clue that would make the dry facts sing. There I might
have the historian Geoffrey Stillwell to help me. On the way I
could have a look at the island that Patrick and those convicts
came to. A route was recommended over the mountains, the
Western Tier, through 'the bush' to an isolated fishermen's
hotel at Moina.

Before I left I was interviewed by a local radio station and
asked (by an Englishman) whether I did not find Australia
'disturbingly monolingual for a multicultural society', a
question which depressed me. I had already begun to enjoy
what Australians were doing to the language, refreshing it, and
did not want them distracted from this process by guilts
imported from England. Also, the question reminded me that
my quest, I supposed, was 'racial', 'cultural', and a search for a
possible distinctiveness, whereas 'multicultural' suggests a
flattening-out. My great-grandmother had presumably fought
the 'multicultural' battle, her children baptised Catholic in the
Protestant monoculture; had insisted on a separate identity
from the Protestant middle-class 'Britishness' at which the
island aimed. Perhaps even my great-grandfather's claim to
connection with the McMurrough Kavanaghs of Borris (if he
made it) – specifically 'old Irish', not Anglo-Irish – could be
seen as an act of resistance to the genteel aspirations of his
English and Scottish neighbours; not snobbery, the opposite, a
refusal to play the class game. A clarity of differing cultural
identities is necessary if the dominant, or majority, culture is to
be enriched; but there has to be a majority culture, which is

not made ashamed to be so, as that question from the radio man suggested he would like it to be. Perhaps I misunderstood him, but, rattled, I went off to hire a car.

After a reluctant departure from secure-feeling Launceston, the first thing noticed was the number of dead animals on the roadside, some of them very large.

In long drives around the island, rarely seeing another car, you pass quantities of dead kangaroos, wallabies, possums, wombats, feral cats. I took to stopping and identifying them. Later, in the south-eastern corner of the island, I saw one that was like no animal I knew: about the size of a long thin cat, its honey-colour fur lightly spotted with round white blobs, like little powder-puffs, and with a pretty, fox-like head. I discovered later it was a south-eastern oull, a marsupial, confined to the island, and now only found in that empty south-eastern corner of it, rarely.

What ill chance had caused that beautiful animal to be run over on an unmade road that saw a car perhaps once an hour, if that? Perhaps the rarity of cars makes animals unwary; but so many are killed it is impossible not to suspect that some are purposely run over, by the kind of high-clearance strengthened vehicles with wide tyres that are often the only ones to be seen on lonely roads. A historical parallel is unavoidable. The carnage is great; perhaps Tasmania thinks it has a bottomless supply of aboriginals, or wishes to destroy them.

The island is certainly wild, and varied, as well as empty of people. Its million inhabitants are mostly congregated in towns. Outside these towns the aloneness can become eerie. This unsignposted road climbed and twisted until it reached black stands of huge pine trees with their heads in dark rags of cloud, and then entered cloud itself. The silence was complete. Some roads on the map just stop, obstructed by mountains or unpenetrated forest. I hoped I was not on one of these, because I found that Tasmania can terrify. Attempts had been made to domesticate it, to tame the spaces with homely names,

Devonport, Launceston, but here the silence is only broken by the shrieks of birds, hoarse and desolate, the language of the landscape. The tarmac gave out, the road became unsealed, rutted, but at last by a sheet of water grey as a fish-scale there was the first building in hours, a clapboard shack with a corrugated-iron roof.

If the first sight of the archives had been reminiscent of Las Vegas, entry into this motel, after the silence, was like the Klondyke. With shouts and roars red-faced men in plaid shirts were punching and slapping each other in amity, five deep at the bar, behind which barmen in singlets dashed and sweated. This was Australian roughness, togetherness, a defiance of silence and dismal bird-shrieks. It was the sort of abandoned public behaviour that in England would be reserved for after closing-time, the pub doors locked, the favoured regulars allowed to roister, an eye cocked for a passing police car. But here there was no thought of policemen; no bosses existed, no favoured classes, no constraints except natural ones; and inside this excess was that secret Australian quality of control, based on mateyness. I still doubted this, doubted whether I could make my request for a room heard, expected my finicking accent to cause a silence, but not at all: someone spotted me behind the rows of drinkers; a key, with a crudely painted wooden tag, was passed between them – 'Here y'are, mate' – and I went out into the sudden dark, walked round the large one-storeyed hut along the wooden walkway of the veranda, and let myself into a brown-painted cold room with four beds in it. I had just time to wonder if I was going to be joined by three of the plaid-shirts when a woman came in with a fan-heater – 'It'll warm you up quicker' – with cornflakes and bread and butter for breakfast.

I did not know how she had seen me in the confusion of the bar, or had been told so quickly the number of my room, but then I understood something: what I had missed in that bar was English pretence: pretence of order, pretence of welcome, pretence of efficiency. Here no one pretended anything, and the system worked. There had been no need for her to bring any of those things; I had not expected them. I now saw there was a cooker, a fridge, an electric kettle of so ancient and complicated a design that I had to sit down and think how it worked, which it did; there was even a cooker. There was, in an inner room I had not noticed, a lavatory and a shower that also worked. The conveniences of a Hilton, without fuss and with untroubled informality in a place which, unlike any Hilton anywhere in the world, was entirely appropriate to where it was, high on a desolate plateau. It was perfect: the Tasmanian bush was poised between untouched wilderness and a comfort that did not reduce that wildness. There was nothing absurd about the Kelloggs or the sliced bread; the first settlers, like soldiers, would have made themselves as comfortable as they could with anything familiar they had to hand. Nor was there, for the moment anyway, much fear that this poise would be disturbed. European and American tourism was too far away to wreck it, or it was too far off the main trail. Tasmania, I thought in the rapidly warming room, could be the last unspoiled attainable wildness in the world.

In the morning the impression of a nearly untouched isolation, its numen still intact, was confirmed. The Great Lake was too vast and chilly an expanse to take colour from the dawn at that time, but a bumpy track led through outcrops with scrub on them, and later came a smaller, by now coloured, lake which had black swans on it that took off and showed white wings. There was a lone fisherman among them, very still and confident, standing up in his boat on the pink water as though he belonged there. He was the last human being for miles, for now came a white and grey forest of primeval gums, eucalypts – there are more than two hundred varieties of these on the island. What is astonishing about them, apart from their ghostly colour, is the way in which they die.

In the tales of the bushrangers, of convicts on the run, they are forever lighting fires in hollow trees so that no one will see the smoke. You wonder how they find conveniently hollow trees so easily. Now I saw that many gums die like this, from the inside. They shed their bark; some, the grey gums, become grey as kangaroos, the white gums become almost spectral, and when they die they bleach even whiter and sag against each other, curved and twisted like dinosaur bones, and sometimes, in their shape and positioning, like dinosaurs themselves. Forests in the beginning of the world must have looked like this, the dying-place of huge beasts.

These dead and dying gum trees are one of the striking features of Tasmania. Because of the way their branches curve, when they fall they land elegantly propped, as though on legs. You see this everywhere, even by themselves in the middle of pasture, huge poised beasts, grey and white, with preying necks upraised.

Once in a while the forest briefly clears and you look down, sometimes very far down, into sculptured pastoral vales, empty, with the brownish, healthy-looking native grass. You pass through moors like the Grampians, and then at last there is tarmac again, and the two-way main road to Hobart, at Bronte.

How do Tasmanians survive the confused cultural references of their place-names? Lake St Clair, Mount Olympus, Derwent Bridge? There is a Brighton nowhere near a beach, a nearly treeless Epping Forest which is near Avoca, the name of a little Irish place serenaded by Tom Moore. Anything, perhaps, to make the place more homely, for vast stretches of it are not homely at all. In a car park by the glacial Lake St Clair a Japanese was photographing a depraved-looking wallaby. In the kiosk food was sold for these animals in paper-bags labelled 'Wallaby Tucker'. There I bought a sandwich and was swooped upon by a crow with a black beak more serious than was comfortable, broad at the base and in no hurry to narrow. It was a black currawong, 'confined to Tasmania', and to placate it I gave it a sandwich. Seeing this, a crowd of them swooped and I took refuge in the car. Among the trees, tree-coloured, were more wallabies like shadows, with dull eyes, exuding the boredom of aeons. In order to avoid that dispiriting gaze you might well feel a psychic need to distance them, to feed them patronising bags of 'Wallaby Tucker', or you might go mad. The original Tasmanians granted spirits to places as well as to animals. They made their world even larger and more powerful than it was by introducing a spiritual dimension which had to be placated. Our way is to try to shrink the world to a size that we hope we can manage, but the motive is the same.

The little bridge over the river Derwent at this point is Wordsworthian; could have been painted by Cotman, but in his painting there would be no place for the baleful currawong, with its demented orange eye. Tasmania has for long stretches been made fertile and hospitable but there is something in it that oppresses the European soul: the way the trees die like prehistoric beasts, the screams and groans and derisions of its birds, the look in a wallaby's eyes. There is even a native animal of such ugliness and ferocity, so nightmare a beast, that no one has found an excuse for it; naturally it is called, almost jokingly, a 'Tasmanian Devil', but its very existence seems to contain a threat. Something in the island resists us, cannot be digested; there is a terror somewhere that we cannot master. Possibly because we have left alive no native inhabitants to translate the place for us, introduce us to it, white men are condemned to be uneasy there for ever.

8

John Mitchel

On the little main road the signpost pointed 'Hobart' one way
and 'Queenstown' the other. Queenstown is where the island
has been 'tormented' into weird shapes and colours by various
kinds of mining. Throughout my stay on the island one of the
first things I was asked was 'Have you seen Queenstown?', as
though it worried people. If I had known this was to be so I
would have gone there, but I felt I could imagine it, and chose
the direction of Hobart.

It was not that I was in search of the safe and the pastoral; it
was because I was after Patrick; and his forebears and
descendants, including me, have managed to avoid contact
with the industrial altogether. This is a limitation because we
have profited from its energies and discoveries, but there it is. I
would have gone to Queenstown only as a *voyeur*. If men have
wrecked the land around there, what is surprising about that?
We are bad news, wherever we go.

By the side of the road, among the dead animals, there was a
little yellowstone monument, almost an altar, on which had
been placed a kind of offering, like those round Lazarian's Well
in Carlow, a row of empty beer bottles. It was marked as 'The
Geographical Centre of Tasmania', erected in tribute to the
early surveyors of the island, and it was pleasant to be told one
had reached the heart of a place so soon. Behind the quasi-altar
was a small reed-filled lake, and through the reeds a man in a
sweat-stained bush-hat carefully, almost silently, nosed his
boat. A pleasant Sunday sight, perhaps, but a man moving as

carefully as that is usually bad news for some other creature. Men moving carelessly too; the pull-in by the monument was littered with animal bodies, presumably pushed there from the road. Among them was one that looked like a large domestic tabby, but it was more sinewy, and in death its jaws were open in a snarl.

For a while the landscape continued to be reminiscent of the Grampians with gum trees. There were the stone-colour, kangaroo-colour sheep, with their small heads. But the chief feature was always the ghostly eucalypts, the way they die, and also the way they grow. Some have leaves rattling in plateaux that are differently angled, and therefore catch the light differently so that they look sculpted. Others have the appearance of having died but show a surprising sprout of green at the highest point; these are called 'celery tops'. Others are indeed dead and have taken on their other life, as white beasts propped on curved legs.

At the little town of Ouse, the river Ouse meets the river Derwent and suddenly the island is genuinely familiar, English; there are imported hawthorn hedges and a smell in the air of orchards. Soon there are indeed orchards, but it is almost a disappointment to come upon them, to find a journey through so many landscapes declining so abruptly into the domestic. But there is another reason for discomfort: you never know when the strange is going to protrude; the soil round the orchard trees, for example, newly ploughed, is a disconcerting and unnatural-looking lavender-pink.

Hamilton (of the orchards) is a small place now, but earlier it was important, and there is a substantial stone hotel – 'Convict-built', it announces on its front. In the bar was a leaflet with a history of this pretty 'English' place. It was wholly built by convicts, gangs of whom were stationed here, together with a flagellator 'whose services were much in demand!' The exclamation mark is evidence of the unease that lies over the island the moment it considers its past. There are enough reasons for this. Outside the hotel is the broad, fertile valley of the Derwent, with its lavender-coloured fields; it was the favourite hunting-ground of the Big River tribe of aboriginals which, even as the chain-gangs – and the flagellator – were at work, was being wiped out. The present inhabitants have such a bloodiness of history to digest, it is no wonder they ignore it, or try to make fun of it with exclamation marks, or try to dig further and further back in the archives, as though trying to reach a time before it all happened.

In the bar that Sunday morning were four men, farm-workers, all small, all glazed after their Saturday night's drinking, on which they were holding an inquest, with relish, in slurred country accents. A fifth man sat alone, announcing to the barman that he wished to remain so, that he did not want to join their drinking-school. He ordered a glass of beer, and another glass in which a large port and a large brandy were mixed; this order he repeated three times within the space of quarter of an hour. It was one o'clock of a Sunday afternoon. I watched with awe.

I listened to the talking four, and watched them. The last thing anyone travelling in Tasmania wants to do is speculate about the continuance of the convict 'stain', especially if he does not consider it a stain at all. Nevertheless there was something queer and distorted, out-of-drawing, about all their faces, and in different ways. They looked like convicts ought to look. I refused to allow this chance impression to impose a stereotype on Van Diemen's Land, but the argument was lost as soon as I admitted to myself that if that connoisseur of physiognomies, of the *comédie humaine*, Fellini, were making a film about penal times he would snap up these four without hesitation as extras for the chain-gang. Nor would he waste them; he would allow the camera to linger, and get his money's worth.

What this proved I did not know. There were those superb, gold-haired children seen in Launceston. Perhaps this country district had received little new blood. Even so, why should petty criminals drawn from all over the British Isles have any physical characteristics in common to pass on to their descendants? It is possible that the prison that was Van Diemen's land might produce some characteristics of behaviour, such as a particular attitude to authority, but it could hardly extend to the creation of ears that stuck out at right angles, of noses disconcertingly too large (or small) for the faces, a setting of the lips that did not seem quite right either. Perhaps that group was a fluke. They were impressive, and a traveller in a novel by Sir Walter Scott, seeing these men at the inn, would certainly have secured his money and looked to his pistols before setting out on the lonely road.

John Mitchel had much to say that was unpleasant about the genetic make-up of the islanders. He farmed fourteen miles from Hamilton on his 'Ticket of Leave': he always put that phrase in inverted commas because he denied the right of the British government to give him such a thing, that government having forfeited its legality because of its misconduct towards Ireland. He was sent to Van Diemen's Land in 1849 for sedition, and the book he wrote there, *Jail Journal*, contains such vivid descriptions of his life in that place, and has made such a potent contribution to Irish nationalism, to 'Irishness', that he is doubly important to this story. He is significantly responsible for the violence in Ireland today because he rationalised the ethos behind it. The use made of him by Irish revolutionaries is, of course, selective. He may have been a 'martyr' for Ireland, but he is wholesale in his contempt for his fellow convicts, including Irish ones. He regarded them, genetically, as less than human: ' "Rural population!" It is almost profane to apply the title to these rascals. All the shepherds and stock-keepers, without exception, are convicts – many of them thrice convicted convicts! There is no peasantry. Very few of them have wives; still fewer families; and the fewer the better.'

He seems torn between his private, patrician disdain and a desire to blame everything on the British government.

> They are friendly to one another – hospitable to travellers (partly because they thirst for news) and otherwise comport themselves partly like human beings. Yet human they are not. Their training has made them subterhuman, preter-human; and the system of British 'reformation discipline' has gone as near to making them perfect fiends as human wit can go. One is perpetually reminded here of that hideous description of Van Diemen's Land, given by a person who knew it well: – 'Let a man be what he will when he comes here, the human heart is taken out of him, and there is given to him the heart of a beast.' What a blessing to these creatures, and to mankind, both in the northern hemisphere and the southern, if they had been hanged!

Mitchel was a brave, intelligent man, but a fierce and cold one. He was a Protestant, as most Irish political leaders have been (a Congregationalist, and a solicitor), and his calm, reasoned advocacy of violence was widely read and digested in the century that followed. There is something implacable about him which, despite his undoubted courage, chills. He was also possessed of a certain stern humour. In 1853, a few miles up the road from the Hamilton hotel (which he visited), he made a point of buying, from the magistrate who had charge of him, the horse on which he intended to escape. He remains the outstanding describer of the island at that time, when Patrick was there, and drops important clues about atmo-sphere. His first landlady in 1849 'took an early occasion of informing me that she "came out free"; which, in fact, is a patent of nobility in Van Diemen's Land. Here, a freeman is a king; and the convict class is regarded just as the negroes must be in South Carolina.' Did that patent run for the Irish free settlers also, one wonders, those without money? He seems to have met few, and his refusal to distinguish between Irish and English convicts does not accord with sentimental Irish legend.

He veers, as anyone does who comes to Tasmania, between a love for the familiarity of the place and a sudden horror, after all, at its foreignness. He likes the sound the river Shannon makes (the Tasmanian one, which runs not far from Hamilton), but, 'The birds have a foreign tongue: the very trees whispering to the wind, whisper in accents unknown to me; for your gumtree leaves are *all* hard, horny, polished as the laurel – besides, they have neither upper nor under side, but are set on with the planes of them vertical; therefore they can never, never let breeze pipe or zephyr breathe as it will, never can they whisper, quiver, sigh or sing, as do the sycamores and beeches of old Rosstrevor.' That is a precise observation, about the leaves and the noise that gum trees make, so he can be allowed the elegiac homesickness, to which he seldom gives way. He can even be forgiven the passages of classicising and quotation that follow, on the subject of rivers and waters; he is writing to pass the time; but he is pulled up, after a lengthy mental bathe in the cultures of distant Europe, like the visitor today, by the island: 'But, behold! plump into the water, just under the bank, tumbles a *Platypus*, uncouth, amphibious quadruped, with broad, duck-like bill; and shrill from a neighbouring gumtree yells "the laughing jackass" – a noisy bird so named by profane colonists. We are in Australia, then!' He had other reminders:

Yes, in Australia indeed! We overtake on our track homeward, a man and a woman – the woman, a hideous and obscene-looking creature, with a brandy-bloated face, and a white satin bonnet, adorned with artificial flowers. She is a pass-holding servant, just discharged from some remote settler's house, and she is going to Hobart Town in custody. The man is a convict-constable; he carries a musket on his shoulder, and his blue frock is girt by a belt, on which hang and jingle a pair of handcuffs. He knows us, and touches his cap as we ride hastily past.

On another occasion, dreamily classicising, asking himself whether a building on the horizon is a Grecian temple, he again crashes back to Australian earth:

Damnation! It is a convict 'barrack'. And as we follow the winding of the road through the romantic glen, we meet parties of miserable wretches harnessed to gravel carts, and drawing the same under orders of an overseer. The men are dressed in piebald suits of yellow and grey, and with their hair close-cropped, their close leather caps, and hang-dog countenances, wear a most evil, rueful and abominable aspect. They give us a vacant but impudent stare as we ride by. I wish you well, my poor fellows; but you all ought to have been hanged long ago!

If only Mitchel could allow himself a spark of sympathy. We are getting almost to like him, despite his hate-filled politics, when he gives himself away by saying things like that. (If ever he had governed Ireland, Ireland might have learned to rue it.) His way of looking at the convicts was doubtless the conventional response of the time, but few things bring home more clearly the hellishness of a convict's life in Van Diemen's Land than the way a man of Mitchel's cultivation and intelligence is nearly unable to regard them as human. How, then, were they regarded, and treated, by lesser men, and by their gaolers? Well might their stare be 'vacant'; it is a relief to learn that at the same time it was still capable of being 'impudent'.

In 1851 his wife and children come out to join him and he has a farm of 200 acres, although still a prisoner. He is happy farming, and rhapsodises about the island, until he again begins to wonder if there is not something *wrong* with the place. He is tempted, short of any other explanation, to put this down to electricity, or the lack of it, in the air:

> There is somewhat stifling to the brain, as well as invigorating to the frame, in this genial clime and aromatic air. A phenomenon for which I strive to account in various modes. One of my theories is the peculiar condition of the atmosphere with respect to electricity. In the three years I have wasted among these hills and woods, there has not been one good thunderstorm . . . the fact is certain, there is more languor, and less excitability among Tasmanians, native or imported, than I have ever witnessed before . . . they are incurious, impassive, quiescent.

That last is astonishingly close to my own impressions of Tasmania (before I read Mitchel). He was making these observations when Patrick was there and I was making some of the same ones more than a hundred years later, so perhaps I was not so far from a sense of Patrick's island after all. For what but 'quiescence' – or acquiescence – was in the bus driver who turned off the video at my request during my first moments on the island, in those obedient pedestrians waiting for the light's permission before they walk, what but 'languor' was to be seen in the slow climb of present-day Tasmanians, so often noticed, from impassive incuriosity into polite alertness? There were more parallels to be discovered, but it was time for another assault on the archives, in what Mitchel called 'that metropolis of murderers, the university of burglary and all subter-human abomination, Hobart Town'.

9

Hobart

In Launceston it had seemed indelicate to mention Hobart, to ask about a good place to stay there. Groups identify themselves by disliking other groups, and between north and south Tasmania there had long been more than a coolness. (When W. G. Grace brought his England eleven to the island they played twenty-two 'Gentlemen of Tasmania' drawn equally from north and south: so that there should be no confusion between them, the south wore red and the north wore white.)

As a result I was disconcerted by what seemed the absence of hotels and, on Sunday, the rarity of passers-by to ask. What few people I saw I stopped, and there it was again, the stare, the bucket going down into the well and slowly wound to the surface, the smile – then the admission that they knew no hotel. It turned out, in order to catch one likely-looking informant, that I had stopped the car outside an hotel, the Hadley-Orient – 'Convict-built' – which I had not noticed (neither had he, for he said he knew of no hotel). I went in; the girl at the desk was making a long telephone call to a friend, examining her nails, so I went out again.

I was hot and tired and had been driving for days. I quartered the centre of town on foot (it is built on the grid principle, and climbs with increasing steepness from the sea towards Mount Wellington). It is the capital of the state and looks it, there are many tall new buildings that shine with glass and steel: a modern metropolis, unlike Launceston ('the entrepreneurial centre of Tasmania', as I was proudly told there), and the high building makes it too similar to other places. My impatient pacing failed to reveal an hotel, so I went back to the car and the original one, which was too grand. The chatting girl had been replaced by a formal young man in a black jacket who led me to a room. By this time I was glad to have anywhere to unpack the chaos of books and pamphlets and notes that had accumulated on the way. He watched with interest while I helplessly allowed these, like a tide, to spread over the room. Perhaps, like everyone in Tasmania, I was dazed by the empty spaces I had passed through. In order to cover this confusion I asked him whether he was English, because of the way he spoke, and this seemed to please him. No, he was not, but had just returned from a spell in London working, among other places, at the Groucho Club. 'Oh,' I said, vaguely. 'Do you know Jeffrey Bernard?' (A columnist of the *Spectator* who often wrote about the place). Indeed he did, indeed, indeed, and smiled at the memory. Did I know Jeffrey? Was I a writer? In which case, perhaps I would prefer a larger room, so that I could spread my papers – which by now had spread themselves across the floor – no extra charge. I said I would so prefer, and he led me to a vast one while we chatted of the Groucho and of people and places that I barely knew, if I knew them at all. The room looked out on St David's Cathedral, which was surrounded by two-storey stone buildings that might have been in Edinburgh, except for their dark red roofs of corrugated iron.

So, as a welcome reminder of his London life, I 'spread my papers', having accepted a false identification with a group (though belonging to none; the reason for the trip) and the sense of inward discomfort that kind of falseness brings, for I knew hardly anything of his Groucho, had the freedom of non-membership and was using the privilege of an assumed membership also: the best of both worlds, like my great-grandfather, perhaps Church of Ireland, his children baptised as Catholics. This reminded me that it was Sunday evening.

Catholicism was my only group membership (not that my

friends were Catholics) and informed my way of looking at the world. Infantilism, sentimentality, evasion? Some of my friends might think so, but over the years it has slowly presented a key to everything, politics, private life, death, art; one that fitted wherever it was tried. The Mass included pain and insisted on praise. I had come to see it as a prefectly constructed dramatic sequence, and was always thrilled, after the pleas for mercy and forgiveness that could sometimes sound so craven, by the *verum et dignum est*, the emphatic, repeated insistence on the necessity to praise, which is a human need, too often forgotten.

Others found faith difficult, or impossible. I, for the moment, found it increasingly easy (it could always be taken away). The easiness sometimes worried me, and in Launceston, over a disgusting pub-lunch, I had asked a historian-priest about this. (I was paying for the lunch, and I regretted its badness; priests, contrary to popular belief, lead hard lives. I wish it had been a better lunch.) I dared ask him the daft question: why did I find faith so easy? He answered without hesitation: 'It usually comes through the mothers.'

He knew as little of my past as I then knew myself. I had not yet learned of Margaret Paul, married to Protestant, possibly indifferent, Patrick, who had her succession of children baptised by Father Butler, there in Launceston. Perhaps she had been a powerful woman, powerful enough, over so long a time, and through the sequence that came after her, to have affected me.

So I went to evening Mass at St Joseph's, Hobart (built, I noted with satisfaction, in 1841, and therefore going strong before Margaret arrived), joined the only social group I almost belong to, slipping in, of course, at the back, and watched the backs of the necks of middle-aged Australian men bellowing lustily and unselfconsciously about the love of God. Australian necks seem more wrinkled than most; perhaps it is the sun, or perhaps Australian haircuts make them more visible. Tough

Australian men with tough Australian voices sang of such mystical things as though it was the most natural behaviour in the world. Anthony Burgess has said that he feels at home 'wherever the sign of the Cross is made' and, although I would not put it like that, I feel the same. I felt at home in that church, with those people, as nowhere else, although I would probably have nothing to say to them once outside it; that is my fault, but it is also the point of our being together in that place.

Of course, nowadays, you have to be careful. At one point a guitar struck up and a single voice began embarrassingly to sing, in the first person singular, about his love for God and God's love for him. I detected a stiffening in the necks in front of me, a suggestion in them that this was something to be endured, a concession to somebody else's taste that would not last long, things would become serious again soon, and meanwhile to remain as still as possible, almost interrupting breathing itself, kept the thing somehow at bay.

We had come to hear the liturgy, a distilled poetry of complete seriousness, which is public and private at the same time. We did not want to hear this solo singer using a popular 'folk' idiom, hitting his quarter-tones, fingering his chords, performing. We did not want to take on the burden of his personality and talent, even if he had any; just as we did not want to take on the personality of the priest who was an impersonal mediator. In his performance of the liturgy – for it is a performance – his personality was irrelevant, and we were set free to think of things larger than personality. The more a church reaches out to the presumed tastes of its people (possibly the priest's private tastes) the more, I suspect, people stiffen and resist. The church should not be the same as the rest of life with another element, sometimes almost apologetically, added. It should be entirely different, familiar yet strange, straining belief. We have enough of 'life', of personality, of being wooed by salesmen of all kinds. We need the *mysterium* and drama of the liturgy, which is at the same time loving: but not the priest's or the guitar-player's 'loving'; God's. In Australia, where there is change, you see the future. Perhaps even that anchor, the Mass, is beginning to slip.

Outside everywhere was shut, and I was reduced to being the sole diner in the vast hotel dining-room. Sometimes when you travel alone you are more alone than you want to be. It was after this evening, approving the good idea Australians have of naming their wines by the grape, that I found in my notebook next morning the only note I had made, and in large letters, 'CABERNET IS O.K.' – inspired perhaps by the rhyme.

The truth is that I had drunk too much of it because I was becoming anxious. I had been more than a week on the island and felt no nearer to what I had come to find. The decision not to define too closely what precisely I was looking for had been deliberate, but no definition seemed to be emerging; although I was becoming more and more interested in the way European life had taken root there and developed. However, everyone to whom I had blurted out my approximate purpose had said that if any man could help me that man was Geoffrey Stillwell, the historian, in Hobart. I had an appointment with him on that Monday.

Before it I went to the docks and found that the new government buildings obscure the first warehouses, built by the army and still standing, but muffled by new façades, as though Hobart wished to bury its past. Later warehouses – 'Convict-built' – have been turned into boutiques and coffee shops. In Australia off-licences are called 'bottle shops'; here they were 'bottle shoppes'. Among the moored boats I tried to book a passage to Port Arthur down the coast, the convict settlement for second offenders which, Robert Hughes says, is best approached through the narrow gap in the high basalt cliffs which is the way the convicts reached it. But at the docks, scene of so much punishment and suffering, there were only brief excursions on offer, trips up the river Derwent – 'Sail with

Cap'n Bob' – and the voyage to Port Arthur was considered too dangerous; poor convicts.

Hobart was going to be tough to dig into; several thick skins had grown over it since Patrick came to the island and it had entered whole-heartedly into the twentieth century. Paradoxically, the difficulty of the place from this point of view helped me to understand that my anxieties were foolish, that I could not possibly expect any place to open up to me, imaginatively, after so many years in which it had wanted to forget its past. Relieved, I went into a white-painted pub, extraordinarily clean and fresh, open to the street, furnished like an expensive cocktail bar. The girl served beer with one hand while she worked a many-buttoned electronic machine with the other, handing out slips. I then understood, to my delight, that it was also a betting-shop; compared to the places recently and grudgingly allowed in England, furtive behind smoked glass, it was a revelation. There was a television set in the corner, sound turned off; men and women came in, bought drinks, bought slips and talked to each other. At a given moment the sound on the television was turned up, not loud, the race was watched, drinks were sipped, no comment was made and talk was resumed. Everyone says that Australians are passionate gamblers, but this was guilt-free gambling made elegant. Australians are civilised; their comportment on the pavements, when driving, in restaurants – in betting-shops – is more restrained and civil than English behaviour. C. J. Koch warns that Tasmanians are special – 'Tasmania is a different place' –but Tasmanians are also Australians.

Australian radio is civilised. In my hotel room, shaving, I had listened to a talk on St Gregory Nazianzen, one of a series on the early church fathers. Before that had been a reading of poems by Southey and Wordsworth, followed by their Lewis Carroll parodies. On the other channels the disc jockeys had a speed and freedom greater than that of ours at home; they even made fun of the advertisements. In their performances there was, however, another note, which caught the attention, required reflection.

Having decided that I could never crack Hobart, not in terms of Patrick, I pushed aside the file loaded with questions about the past with which I was soon to badger Stillwell, ordered another beer, and gave myself permission for a few generalisations about Australia, as it was, here and now.

Those disc jockeys: they were male, and often had a female sidekick whose function was, audibly, to goggle at her male colleague's flights of fancy, calculated lunacies, insults, jokes; to attempt to restrain him, and fail. It was a form of ritualised sex-play, male centred.

This also happened in private. The men joshed each other and the women, for the most part silent, looked on in a theatrical round-eyed wonder at the outrageousness of their menfolk, thus inspiring them to further heights; yet the men deferred to the women, occasionally touching them, squeezing their hands almost secretly for reassurance, as though wanting to be mothered as well as admired. Australia had needed Germaine Greer.

There was something in that male joshing that was reductive, an insistence on basics that was a form of bullying. To anyone trying to be serious it was saying, 'Come off it, mate! All you want is a bundle of money, a beer in your fist and a willing Sheila. Like everyone else!' The right to any other kind of conversation had to be fought for in the face of this aggressive scepticism, the lips of the opponent (for such he was, beneath the joshing) pursed in a silent raspberry. This, I thought, could wear you down. It could not be easy to step out of the group, the herd, in Australia. It could not be easy to be different, or any sort of artist, what with gentility on the one hand and this aggression on the other.

Yet the country was producing talents distinctively Australian. Perhaps it was these twin pressures that made them what they were. Sydney Nolan goes behind gentility, back to the bush and the bushrangers, Arthur Boyd floats in the localised surreal, Les A. Murray writes poems with titles like 'A Dream of Wearing Shorts Forever'. Any pretentiousness is knocked out early. If they want to be artists it has to be with no nonsense about it. So much the better.

Then there is the matter of the Great Australian Pause. They frequently leave a beat of three after you have finished speaking, before they reply, as though anxious not to tread on the echo heard on the satellite telephone to England. You feel your remark is reaching them through the same vast space. Nor do they fiddle and fidget while you speak, they sit as still as obedient pupils in class. This is disconcerting to anyone not used to it; you begin to falter, lose your way, while they wait. At first I thought it was due to the difficulty of my English accent, or it was a form of politeness to a stranger. But I heard that silence formalised, as it were, on Australian radio to such ludicrous effect (on English ears) that sometimes I burst out laughing in my hotel room. It seemed to constitute a genuine cultural difference, an altogether different interpretation of silence. For example, if a politician interviewed on the radio says in answer to a question, 'It is entirely untrue that a large part of Queensland has been sold to the Japanese', and his reply is followed by a gap of three beats, that gap, in Britain, would mean 'You are a liar!' At least it would convey incredulity and the next question would almost certainly begin with an exasperated 'But . . .' It has no such inference in Australia. The prolonged pause after a recorded report on a news bulletin is equally comic to an English ear. Such a lengthy silence is allowed before someone says, 'That was Red Harrison, from Beirut', you have time to fear there has been some mistake, to imagine the presenter mouthing to the producer behind his glass window, 'What sort of crap was that?' Or the producer signalling wildly, in dumb show, 'Wrong report!'

Then there is Australian beer. In this delightful bar betting-shop, while occupied with these reflections, I had made the experiment of having three small glasses of the three kinds of beer on offer. There were always three, served into little glasses from curved metal taps: Castlemaine, Fosters, and the local brew of wherever you happened to be. Great care was taken to discover which one you wanted and to make sure you received it: a hand was put on the selected tap and your order checked, as though if a mistake was made you might throw the beer in the barman's face. The experiment had confirmed what I suspected: all three tasted the same.

But it was time to collect up that file loaded with questions and possibly irrelevant photostats, time to collect up energy.

What had been most exhausting about the trip was the necessity to become a sort of salesman of questions. You had to find the right person, ask the right question and do so until their interest was engaged and they were inspired to help you further; and this had to be done in a country alert to, and suspicious of, any attempt to charm. Nevertheless you had to try to charm because you were, after all, asking for favours. I knew I would have to perform in this way, before I left England, and it was one of the reasons I had come alone. You cannot try to make yourself of interest under the eye of someone who knows what you are like normally. Priests I had found entirely impervious. Like good doctors or good social workers they remained available and detached, they had no favourites. At first baffled by their even calm, I came to be impressed, and comforted. There are still good priests.

For other kinds of interview I had to psych myself up, like an athlete, or a candidate, and this was the Big One.

I therefore walked up the hill to the library, to the appointment, feeling nervous. We met almost at the door and I sensed within seconds that Geoffrey Stillwell, the man I had been waiting to meet for months, was not going to be able to help me at all. He was in a way too scholarly, too knowledgeable, for my small questions. Instead of being disappointed I surprised myself by beginning internally to laugh. I now knew I had never believed that Patrick was in the archives.

In appearance and manner he was like the nicer, dottier kind of Oxbridge don: chubby, spectacles pushed to the top of his curly head. He knew so much of his subject that he almost free-associated; any question could send him off in any direction and often, it seemed, in many.

'It's all very well Chris Koch putting you on to me, I haven't done any research since these bloody microfiche things came in. Seen these letters from Fitzroy, captain of the *Beagle*? Keen on weather. Chap here writing a history of the Australian weather-patterns in the 1840s. There he is. How are you getting on?'

Other scholarly-looking men sat at tables and called out questions to him as he passed (he was on his way to discuss his trousers with the doorman). 'Mr Stillwell, Mr Stillwell. Can you tell me about the Port Arthur Chief Engineer. 1841?'

'Warburton? A rascal. Ask McFee. Used to spell his name "Mc", now it's "Mac". I still spell it the same, though. You, Mr Kavanagh. Yes. What can I do for you? Let's see. Well, we'd better go up to the archives. Haven't been there for years. Not my field. Just have to see Bill for a moment. Come on.'

With the commissionaire, he debated whether he should or should not collect his trousers from the dry cleaner's to take with him to Melbourne tomorrow. Tomorrow? I did not have the attention of this well of information for long. You never knew; one lucky question dropped, and he might bring up a clue.

I followed him to the lift, thinking of questions; there was so little time. He appeared to have difficulty with its operation, or affected to. It was a matter of keys, security, not everyone was allowed up to the archives in case they were tracing someone's convict ancestry, or hoping to erase their own. He introduced me to the people in charge (it was indeed quieter than

Launceston) and lurked while I discovered that my grandfather was not on the government list of births in Tasmania.

'Impossible!'

'Look for yourself.' He shrugged. 'Parish priest was slack.'

'It was Father Butler.'

'Dean Butler? He was a careful priest.' He shrugged again,
and said, in a way that encouraged me. 'Must have got lost.'

This suggested that a real historian is resigned to *lacunae*,
whereas an amateur tends to think they must be his fault. He
knew the name and style of the Catholic priest in Launceston in
the 1850s. He knew everything about Tasmania except what I
wanted to know: why Henry Dowling had helped to pay
Patrick's fare. 'Must have been money in it for Dowling,
knowing him', was all he would venture. If Patrick had stayed
he would have known all about him, his children, their
circumstances, addresses, successes, scandals. But Patrick had
left the island (I suspected, and later it turned out to be so)
about 1866, because after that date he no longer owned a house
in Launceston; just about the time clear traces of him might
have been recorded. Whatever I was looking for was not in the
archives, or not much. It had to be in the island itself, where he
had spent a quarter of a century.

As for the archives, Stillwell voiced my unspoken yearning.
'What you need is a research assistant. Trouble is,' he went on,
'most of 'em are no good. Can you think of anyone, Margaret?'
This to the chief archivist, who had already found me, in
seconds, the passenger list of the *Arab* and the reference number
of the document that stated no person of the occupation of
groom was recorded as entering the island in 1842. Stillwell
was now telling me that I was expected in Sydney, by Chris
Koch and others; in awe of him the archivist was waiting for
him to stop.

'Do you think Anne Rand could help Mr Kavanagh?' she
suggested, shyly.

'Anne. Perfect. Best in business. Ring her at once. Beer?'

I felt my troubles were perhaps coming to an end.

He took me up the steep hill to the house he shared with his sister. Surprisingly, as we climbed away from the sea, the houses became older. I would have expected towns to begin around the wharves, as they had elsewhere in the world, but down there was probably a convict scene and the better-off built well away from it, on the heights. The house was of neatly cut yellow stone, apparently one-storey, but as so often there was a storey below, cut into the hillside. It was the kind of house, with a cared-for but pleasantly overgrown garden, that any scholar might live in: North Oxford – English – Tasmanian.

'You're a man with one idea, aren't you? You won't let it alone. I like that. I'm like that. I didn't help you at all, did I? I'm out of that world now. It's a difficult field.'

It was. He had helped me more than he could know. I was free: I had help in the archives. I could explore the island.

10

A Trunk in the Attic

Let a present-day Tasmanian talk about Hobart, Tasmania and its past:

Here is Franklin Square, the town's nineteenth century heart; its big old plane trees out in leaf. I look up at Sir John Franklin and inwardly salute him, as I always do. Chart in hand, the doomed explorer stands on his plinth in the middle of the ornamental pool, a seagull perched as usual on his bald head, which wears a snowy cap of seagulls' droppings. Other gulls wheel and cry about him like the souls of his sailors, lost in the ice of the North West Passage. We are fond of Franklin, in Tasmania; he was kindly, and one of our good governors; the information has been transmitted down the generations.

When Franklin and Lady Jane made their overland expedition to the wild west coast, they were brought back to Hobart on the schooner *Eliza*, under the command of my paternal great-great grandfather, Captain James Hurburgh, who settled in Van Diemen's Land in 1837. The past is like a trunk in the attic here, very close at hand; ancestors are not far away.

That is C. J. Koch, novelist, born in Hobart. It is true that the past feels close at hand, but it is difficult to put your hand upon it; perhaps this is because it is surrounded by poisonous air. You cannot reach back to settler ancestors without having to push through a miasma of punishment cells, flogging triangles, sullen and stunned chain-gangs, because that is what free settlers lived among, perhaps pretending not to see. But they did see, because as soon as Tasmania ceased to be a prison island there is plenty of evidence that all its citizens, whatever their pasts, showed resentment at what had been done there, dismantled gallows and gaols. Also, of course, pushed to the back of their minds, was the fate of the natives, who soon no longer existed.

Another Australian writer, H. A. L. Porter – from Queensland, not from the island, which perhaps makes it easier for him to do so – seizes upon the gothic aspect: 'Van Diemen's Land, a ugly trinket suspended on the world's discredited rump . . . . It was the privy of London . . . turnkey ridden and soldier-hounded. No one returned over the crags except bushrangers, crazed from suppers of human flesh, and chattering a litany learned in a hinterland of horror.' There are thick strands in the island's history that seem to demand to be written about in that fashion (alas), but Tasmania can never have been 'ugly'. Native-born Koch is calmer:

> The entire landmass of Australia – most of it flat and very dry – lies north of latitude forty. Tasmania, filled with mountains and hills, and containing more lakes than any comparable region except Finland, lies south of latitude forty, directly in the path of the Roaring Forties. It genuinely belongs to a different region from the continent: in the upside-down frame of the Antipodes, it duplicates north-western Europe, while the continent is Mediterranean and then African. So it was very easy, in what was once Van Diemen's Land, for our great-grandfathers to put together the lost totality of England.

Of England, perhaps, but not, surely, of Ireland: the Irish who had voluntarily left home had done so because they found

it barely impossible to live there, so badly was it governed –
Edmund Burke, William Cobbett, Alexis de Toqueville and
plenty of other contemporary observers were in agreement
about that – and also because, on account of that mis-
government, it was in a state of growing economic chaos. A
population of five million in 1800 had swelled to eight million
by 1840, resulting in hopelessly uneconomic subdivision of
what little land the ordinary Irish themselves possessed, and
their consequent overreliance on the potato. Sporadically,
throughout the century, there had been famines, and the Great
Famine was only four years away when Patrick decided to
leave in 1841. News of that calamity would feed not a 'lost
totality' of Ireland but a defiant sense of national identity, a
mythology of all that went to make up 'Irishness', on the other
side of the world. A central ingredient of this self-consciousness
would be – because of the priests, because of Cardinal Cullen
and his men – Roman Catholicism.

The myth was not new, but this was new and fertile ground
for it to grow in. *Hiberniores ipsis Hibernis*, 'more Irish than the
Irish': the Latin phrase had a whiff of the medieval about it,
suggesting that there had been a clear flavour of Irishness for
centuries. Perhaps there had been, but recently it has been
pointed out (by an Irishman, of course) that there is no trace of
that phrase before the 1770s, so maybe it was only then that the
myth (and a myth can contain a truth more potent than facts)
was deliberately putting down roots into an imagined past.

A powerful contributer to the political direction of the myth,
John Mitchel, was not a Catholic. He would have scorned the
myth's sentimentalities and religiosities, but it was his
(apparently) clear-headed espousal of violence as the only
solution for Ireland that rang through the Irish world. This
was by this time a wide one, and scattered. Daniel O'Connell
believed in legality, but once his 'delusion of moral force' was
put out of the way, said Young Irelander Mitchel, 'there is a
chance of my countrymen seeing, what is solemn truth, that for

Ireland's "grievances", her families, her party-spirit, her packed juries, her exterminations, there is but one and all-sufficient remedy, *the edge of the sword.*'

The italics are his, and these are almost the first words of his *Jail Journal*. Few of his colleagues agreed with him, but he happens to be an eloquent writer and his book entered Irish consciousness, became part of the sensibility that led to the Easter Rising in 1916 and on from that. It is said it is still to be found, well thumbed, in most Republican households; even if it is not there, the drift of its contents has been learned by heart.

Jail Journal is hardly known in mainland Britain, but the call it makes has haunted British political life for a century, and looks likely to go on doing so, until some British Secretary of State takes time off to read and ponder it. Then he might stop talking publicly of 'thugs' and 'murderers' and admit that he is dealing with zealots, maddened by myth and Mitchel, with a bit of Marx added: a potent mixture. The myth is the most powerful ingredient, founded as it is on old grievances. As some wise man said, 'People are not driven violently to oppose governments because of fears of enslaved grandchildren, but by memories of enslaved grandfathers.'

Memories, in the minds of people long dead, are difficult to weigh. They were in the air of the time, in Patrick's air, and they are in the air of Tasmania still, as Koch suggests, thinned by the passing years and the implacable, waiting quality of the island itself, which seems to be sitting it out until all human beings leave. But to some of these memories Mitchel is a key.

Even if its politics were removed, which is impossible, *Jail Journal* would remain, as Koch says, one of the best things in colonial literature: 'Most of the descriptions we have of early Tasmania are by limited or prosaic men. But with Mitchel, we are looking at the early scenes and the first settlers of the island through the filter of a genuinely poetic imagination; pictures of a society at the edge of a wilderness by an impassioned activist and man of action with the sensibility of an artist.' Koch was therefore understandably thrilled to find his ancestor, Captain Hurburgh, described by Mitchel.

> We made our way this morning to the head of the D'Entrecasteaux Channel, where it communicates by a narrow passage with the great Storm Bay – took a pilot on board at this passage, a little dark man, at whom I gazed as narrowly and curiously as ever did Abel Jans Tasman at the first Australian savages he saw, or they at Abel. But indeed our little pilot was a mere Carthaginian in tweed pantaloons and round jacket; and he came down to his boat from a neat white cottage on a hill, with a greensward lawn sloping from its door to the boat-pier, and some sweet-briar hedges protecting and adorning its garden.

The pilot was Captain Hurburgh, an early Australian, but to the haughty captive, Mitchel, 'a mere Carthaginian', representative, that is to say, of the discredited oppressive power. Koch, of course, liked this mention by Mitchel of his ancestor because it brought the past even closer to hand; the 'neat white cottage on a hill' had been his childhood home. And I was delighted, later, to learn that Patrick had some sort of connection with Mitchel, indirectly, in circumstances to do with Mitchel's escape. This was a powerful indication of the atmosphere Patrick lived in.

We must also remember the air that Michael breathed. From this distance we can disagree with his advocacy of violence, and deplore the pestilence it has bred. But a few days before Mitchel reached Hobart and encountered the 'Carthaginian' pilot, somebody smuggled a copy of the London *Times* into his prison-cabin, and he copied something from it into his *Journal*. It concerns the harsh punitive measures considered necessary in Ireland at that time (in the midst of a famine which was killing hundreds of thousands of people). It is either ironic or incredible; possibly proof of Sydney Smith's opinion that at the mention of the very name of Ireland Englishmen invariably took leave of their senses. ' "Law" ', said the *Times*, 'has ridden roughshod through Ireland of late: it has been taught with bayonets, and interpreted with ruin. Townships levelled to the ground, straggling columns of exiles, work-houses multiplied and crowded, express the full determination of the legislature to rescue Ireland from its slovenly barbarism, and to plant the institution of this more civilised land.' If the writer was using irony, it is significant that the alert Mitchel failed to notice.

The atmosphere of a time, its air, its tone, has somehow to be imagined if the time is to be understood, and its directions can only be gauged by small things, like feathers floating in it. For example, almost everyone who arrived from England to take up public appointments remarked on the greed of the colonists, their obsession with money. Was this English anti-colonial snobbery? One such official, during Patrick's time on the island, went to the theatre in Hobart and found himself, 'squeezed into impatience by the crowd and half-poisoned by the smell of stale tobacco, foul breath and unwashed frowzy bodies proceeding from a dense mass of vulgar, spirit and beer drinking, oily haired knaves who pressed in without mercy.' It is not surprising, if such was the tone, that Tasmanians in return did not think much of their imported public officials.

Nevertheless, what continues to surprise is the degree of the European 'normality' of life there.

Above the once-crowded docks, now more or less empty – 'Sail with Cap'n Bob' – above the grey freestone warehouses the convicts built, which now hold the smart little boutiques and cafés and 'bottle shoppes', is Battery Point: quiet, rather elegant, with rows of old houses, one of which has been turned into a museum and contains much of its original furniture. It astonishes, the way a reasonable well-to-do islander around the 1840s, could somehow gather together the bits and pieces, some of them locally made, with which he would have furnished his home in Cheltenham, or Tunbridge Wells; because the traveller is always conscious of the other history of the island. Below that comfortable English-seeming house, the convicts were building the warehouses; new convicts would be arriving, emerging chained and blinking from their holds; not far away would be the punishment cells, the flogging-triangles, the public gallows, and all this compounded by the sense of being surrounded by a wilderness, and on the far side of the globe. Yet in ths house there are barometers to be tapped, the grandfather clock reassuringly ticking, and the cane-bottomed armchair with its hand-embroidered velvet cushion. Such domestic order, in an island by no means settled: even among the free population, at its most responsible, all sorts of disorder and disputes were going on, in a struggle for its soul.

You can almost see English and European history compressed and re-enacted within the compass of a few years of the history of the island. Its religion was Church of England, but the other sects, including the Roman Catholics, wanted their own churches and forms of education. As the various churchmen and educators in Britain became aware of this they began to send out higher-powered figures to take charge and give direction. These were naturally resented by earlier-come pastors and teachers, who had struggled to build whatever spiritual orderliness the island had so far achieved and, in the process, had probably taken on some of its wildness, had become 'Australian'.

For example, when the Roman Catholic (English) Bishop Willson came out from England in 1844, he found two Irish priests already in the colony. Father Butler was probably already safe from interference in distant Launceston, but Father Therry was in Hobart (praised by the Irish bushranger Martin Cash, whom Therry visited daily in his condemned cell). Bishop Willson pronounced Father Therry 'a great and good man' (as Martin Cash had done), and required him to hand over the deeds of his church, St Joseph's: the one which had featured the folk-singer on my first night in Hobart, the one I had been pleased to see had been built in 1841, and therefore well established before Willson and the devout Margaret Kavanagh reached the island. It was not as well established as all that. Bishop Willson discovered that Father Therry's church debts were considerably greater than he had expected; 'Whereupon Father Therry', Lloyd Robson says, 'coolly informed his bishop that if Willson did not accept the debts he could not have the deeds to Saint Joseph's. This dispute lingered on for another thirteen years, the point unsettled, with factions along national lines forming round the Englishman Willson and the Irishman Therry.' Another suggestion of the Irish nationalist tone of the world in which Patrick moved.

Bishop Willson managed to extract a promise of a huge donation, £10,000, from a Roderick O'Connor, newly converted to Catholicism, and, despairing of St Joseph's, built himself his own cathedral further up the road. The second version of this is still there, and it is where I discovered in the news-sheet why there was no record of my grandfather's birth. The first version of this church proved to have been so badly built (the construction supervised by a pupil of Pugin's) that it was unsafe to go inside it; the walls and columns had been left hollow. It is to be hoped that the men who built this rival to Father Therry's church were not his Irish parishioners.

There were not only disputes among the Catholics. The Anglican Bishop Nixon had a difference with one of his clergymen over the liturgical use of St David's Cathedral, which lay so elegantly and reassuringly outside my hotel window. He went so far as to padlock the door against the Reverend Bedford but he, a Van Diemen's Land old-timer, knew all about padlocks and had it picked in no time. This argument went as far as the Colonial Office in London, because it involved questions of revenue, and proved so complex in church law that the Colonial Office was grateful to hand it over to the Archbishop of Canterbury.

All this may appear ludicrous today, and probably it sometimes was. But men had come to the island either to better themselves or to be punished. These priests, of whichever denomination, were struggling to give seriousness and purpose to the lives of all the inhabitants. If the prisoners were as brutalised as was often claimed, if the free settlers were as brutally greedy, the role of the churches was all the more significant. Thirty years before, the island had nearly sunk into barbarism; this building of churches, even these arguments, represented stages in a huge advance. Even the barometer to be tapped, the embroidered cushion, were not just symptoms of the genteel, they were triumphs over darkness.

Of course religion, or rather church-going, would be used by many as a passport to the 'respectable', as it always has been. Early commentators are all agreed that, after money (the accumulation of which is a part of the process) respectability was the free colonists' ruling passion. By now Anne Rand was coming up with scraps of information which suggested that Patrick had few ambitions in this direction.

Perhaps respectability is an English and Scottish pre-occupation, rather than an Irish one. Yet there are such things as 'lace-curtain Irish' in America, and it occurs to me to wonder whether my mother was one of these – as a young girl she had taught in an aunt's dancing-school in Philadelphia. It is true that as a child she had disliked leaving Edinburgh to visit her O'Keefe cousins in Roscommon, because she found farming dirty, although there was one cousin, Cornelius, whom she loved. A few years ago those cousins remembered with delight 'little Agnes', at the turn of the century, dancing to the fiddle in the cottage where they still lived. Devout and Catholic, she had no indiscriminate love for priests (unless they were unworldly) or for the Irish – which I always thought to be particularly Irish of her. Perhaps her hopes in life were disappointed. She had married my father when he was a medical student with a private income. In the end he did not become a doctor, the income ceased, and hard times followed. She had always wanted security, but not, I think, respectability. As for me, she decided at some stage and for some reason that I was entirely unsuited to the ways of 'this cruel world' (as she would have put it) and this was her highest accolade. Thenceforth she regarded me with a degree of uncritical and to some extent uncomprehending love which is probably the strongest part of my inheritance. Perhaps faith does indeed 'come through the mothers'. But, no, she had no wish to be 'respectable'; if she had she would not have married my father.

As for Patrick, he seemed determined to avoid any category whatever. It was Anne Rand who unearthed an earlier census form, of 1848, in which he claimed to be Roman Catholic. To move in public from Roman Catholicism to membership of the Church of Ireland (which he put down in 1851) in the space of three years suggests a detachment from these quarrels (to say the least) unusual for the time. Meanwhile his successive children were being baptised by Father Butler, and he and Margaret even appear on the small roll of the especially devout, members of Father Butler's 'Rosary Circle', who met together to pray during the week, beyond the call of duty, which, outside the circle, was certainly not 'respectable'. On this earlier census form, as on the other, he confessed to no trade or occupation. On another document, to do with a house, he claimed, unhelpfully, to be a 'dealer'. On yet another, when he took over the house of a baker he cheerfully said he was a baker. Perhaps 'no Irishman takes seriously what he puts on a piece of government paper'. I was predisposed to like him, and now I began to suspect a sense of humour. Of course, I knew I was inventing him, but he was forcing me to, as he had in a way forced the census-takers, and the attorney's clerks to whom he gave all the other information, or non-information.

11

A Tour of the Island

In Hobart it seemed necessary to plunge into possibly relevant offices and ask questions. To explain the questioning I claimed to be a journalist and so was offered brochures about local handicrafts, and fishfarms, and vineyards – 'Bill and Lynn welcome you to Roseacre' – but I was following my nose and it did not lead me in these directions. Town trades were also boosted, and Mure's Fish Restaurant on Battery Point was often mentioned. I had to eat so I went to look for that.

Hobart is almost sinisterly quiet at night: you hear your footsteps echo. The restaurant turned out to be in an old, private-looking house like the one nearby with the barometer and the embroidered cushion. This one had an inconspicuous sign and a locked door, on which was written 'Please ring the bell'; the risk was of being trapped in an empty room, and I had had enough of my own company. Like my great-grandfather, I preferred not to commit myself, and wandered down to the docks where there were at least seagulls, calling out like the souls of Franklin's sailors. Under the docklights they were making an extraordinary noise, even for gulls. They had the extra harshness of all Tasmanian birds, as though they had to be louder to make themselves heard across the wastes.

There were the pleasure-boats bobbing, where the convict ships had moored, and the whalers with their captive aboriginal women. Now it was 'Sail with Cap'n Bob', but the gulls, at least, were wild. They were behaving strangely, quarrelling in one place, on the ground, near the door of a parked car. I tried to see why and they flew away, shrieking. There was nothing on the ground at that spot except tarmac. They had seemed to be mobbing one gull which stood in their centre. I moved back into the shadows and they returned to the same spot, including the unpopular gull, which stood in their midst as before; it was exactly the same spot, same car, same door. Their wildness, and within it some sort of inexplicable order, was oddly comforting. God alone knew what Antarctic spaces these creatures had traversed. Hobart docks then, now, were the same to them; they were the original inhabitants, and the only creatures to be seen.

There was one lit-up building at the end of the docks which might contain people; it turned out to be a restaurant, also owned by the Mures, who were both present; both English, and *le tout Hobart* seemed to be eating there. One man was being televised as he nearly did so; again and again he raised a forkful, from an entire fish, almost to his lips, pronouncing it excellent, then the director called 'Cut!' and after a while he did it again. The fish's eye grew duller under the television lights, and the man looked glazed too; the lens puts a kind of shellac on the faces of those people who stare too often into it. I remembered the ordered wildness of the gulls, and re-membered D. H. Lawrence: 'as for *people*, they are the same anywhere.' I wanted to see more of the wildness of the island, the gulls had reminded me of it; it might bring nearer the present Patrick had known, but I wanted to see it anyway.

Shortly afterwards, when I flew to the south-west wilder-ness, Rex the pilot dipped his wing over Hobart, using it like an index-finger to point at a white house alone on a green promontory: 'That's the Mures' house. You know? The restaurant people?' It was the old sea-pilot's house, Captain Hurburgh's, 'with a greensward lawn sloping from its door to the boat-pier'.

We flew along the coast of the island, over a blue and green sea, the red basalt columns of Tasmania to our right,

Antarctica to our left. Between the two was the occasional green, sun-gilded island; not the rain-green of Ireland, but the sandy-tinctured green of the rich native grass. I had to admit, although I had been determined not to think so, that Tasmania does keep reminding you: 'Don't kid yourself. You may think you're in the Home Counties, in Normandy, in Orkney. You are not. You are at the end of the world.'

Even the thought of the English Mures was puzzling in the context of this loneliness. What could their lives be like, apart from work, although they probably worked all the time? Were they there to make their pile and go home? Perhaps they would stay. He was a keen fisherman, and clearly it was a good place to fish. Perhaps the whole of the Antipodes was for physical people, fishers, surfers, skiers, sun-worshippers, cooks, not for metaphysical people at all, and this made all my questions irrelevant. Perhaps the infant intellectual, Peter Conrad, had been right to burst into tears when he thought how far away he was – from somewhere.

The coast unreeled, inlets, cliffs, wave-washed sandy bays. Rex said he never tired of it; he could fly along it every day, it was a privilege, it was so beautiful. Was it? It was certainly handsome – fox-red bastions of cliff, white breakers, green sea, sharp green mountains with dark wisping mists among them – 'as for *people*, they are the same anywhere' – but people leave interesting fingerprints and here there were none and never had been.

We landed on one of the few flat places, to pick up a bush-walker, near a mountain called Melalucca, which is also the name of the gorse-like grey scrub which covers the bog. It is a strange plant; given a chance, out of the wind (and it clearly had little chance here), it can grow into a quite considerable papery-barked tree, called the ti-tree (or tea-tree; they seem unable to make up their minds about the spelling). Here it just about managed to scratch your calves. The winds, like the stars, seem upside-down in Australia: it is the wind from Antarctica, the south wind, that is to be feared. But here they also had a dreaded north wind, which channels through a gap in the mountains with such force that a single stunted Huon pine was stripped of needles on its north side, although on the south side they still managed to cling on; little outcrops were scoured bare on the north side but scrub grew on the other, an exactly straight line dividing the naked rock from the scrubby growth. Nevertheless, people lived in that place: tin-miners, three of them.

The little airstrip on the bog, surrounded by green mountains, was made of brilliantly white quartz, spoil from the mines. Two of these miners came walking to meet us: a middle-aged English couple in woolly hats (the English were cropping up everywhere). They had built their shack themselves and brought all they needed in by boat, eighteen hours by sea from Hobart, along a coast that even the whalers had feared; fifty miles of mountain between them and the nearest settlement. They seemed to find it normal. They had a JCB digger for the open-cast mine and this charged their batteries, so they had electricity. They even had a Calor gas freezer. The bush-walker had not been walking at all, he had been staying with them, and I was curious to know how they lived, what they ate. 'Oh, just the usual sort of things,' he said, 'like you'd eat anywhere.' There seemed a conspiracy to make this isolation commonplace.

Tin-mining here looked easy enough, if messy. You scrape off the surface bog, pan the quartz underneath, and the metallic grains sink to the bottom: tin, sometimes gold. It is like black sand, but very heavy, a jamjar-ful you have to hold with two hands.

It was pleasant enough at this season, a wet moor surrounded by range after range of mountains, but Rex in his baseball cap kept examining the sky. 'We've got time, I think,' he said doubtfully, quizzing a slab of dark cloud that was slowly inserting itself between two mountains, low, putting itself between us and the direction of Hobart.

On duck-boards over the soggy ground we made our way up

a small slope and then we looked down on a little Grecian grove of ti-trees, man-ferns (which are as big as trees) and myrtles, by a crystal creek. In a hollow sheltered from the wind, almost hidden by foliage in that place otherwise wholly bare above knee-height, was a red-painted Nissen hut belonging to Denny, the other miner, who had lived there since 1945. He was away in Hobart and the walker wanted to pick up something from his house so we went in. There was a notice, 'Please do not close the door until you have checked that birds are out'; wild birds went in and out of his hut. Outside it I had noticed that a wren-like bird with a ridiculously long tail had not startled as we passed. We had heard parrots in the grove, but only glimpsed them. There was another kind of bird, very tame, with startling scarlet underparts. Afterwards I found it was disappointingly called 'beautiful firetail'. If you are going to have to name a bird like that in the Australian bush you might as well call it 'redarse' – but Tasmanians are not like that.

In the wilderness Denny had created a tiny Arcadia. The only reminder of the lateness of the season were the rotted heads of his dahlias. His hut was partitioned into rooms, the divisions stopping at head height, and there were shelves of thumbed paperbacks and a radio mended with sellotape. He had taught the birds not to be afraid of him; perhaps we could get back into some sort of accord with the natural world if we moved far enough away from our fellow men – and were tough. He had rigged himself up a wind-gauge, like a meccano Eiffel Tower which just dared to poke its head above the low, wind-contorted heads of the ti-trees, and he charged his batteries through the little spinning spoons on top. Frequently it registered winds of over a hundred miles an hour; anything higher than that and it fell over.

Rex took a look at the sky and said we had better hurry. We flew back below the peaks through dark mist; Rex, at the controls, kept turning to talk to me in the back seat and I wished he wouldn't. When we landed outside Hobart and Rex switched off the engine a lark was singing above us, in English, the first bird on the island I had heard use that language; perhaps larks had been imported, like hawthorn hedges and apple trees, and I was notably pleased to hear it. I was European, probably with more opportunity to remain so than Patrick had had; but I wanted to see more of the non-European wildernesses of his island. I wanted to see the rainforest.

That is further to the west, mid-island; he must have felt it at his back like a draught, when he was in Launceston. Now the hydro-electric engineers have cut a road some way into it, and this I went to find, breaking the journey at the Amaroo Motel, New Norfolk.

Motels are curious places, at least they are in Tasmania; perhaps they are everywhere. Because each 'suite' has its own front door, and you are supposed to park your car outside that door, each one looks out through a large window on to the courtyard car park and therefore, in your 'suite', unless you want to be peered at by each new arrival, you have to draw your curtains and live by electric light, which can lower the spirits.

I had some notes to write up and some documents copied by Anne Rand to look at, and when I was finished I peered through the curtains and found it was dark. The place was entirely quiet. There had been no new arrivals. I knocked at the door marked 'Office' and was lucky enough to find a youth who was on the point of disappearing. I felt I was lucky to catch him in time, because he seemed the only inhabitant.

He told me that the main street of New Norfolk was just up the hill. This did not look likely because the hill was dark with unlit houses set back from the road, and there was no glow of light at the top. However, I climbed, in a silence so great I began to feel furtive; it was about seven o'clock. Sure enough, at the top was a dimly lit square of grass with a street of the usual pillared, arcaded shops of one storey leading off it. These were all shut except a grocer's on a corner, who was Greek. There was nowhere you could eat. Without birds, it was all much lonelier than Denny's cabin. There was a pub, which I went into; three men stood inside, who stopped talking. I chose one of the three beers from the three curved taps: Castlemaine, Fosters and here, I think, the local one was called Cascade. As the girl began to turn a spigot one of the men stopped her quickly – 'He said Cascade!' (or Castlemaine, or Fosters) – and I swear she blushed, seemed genuinely put out. There is something for the anthropologist to examine in that importance of beer choice. I did not dare to discuss it with the three men, the matter clearly went too deep. They would be unlikely to agree that all three beers tasted the same. Even to mention it might break some taboo, and the tribesmen might decide to break me. So I sloped back down the dark hill, resigned to a supperless evening in the goldfish-bowl of my 'suite' at the Amaroo Motel.

Once again, Tasmania was to spring a surprise, and prove that I was still nowhere near getting the hang of that familiar/unfamiliar place. On my way to my room (the motel was quieter than a graveyard, where there might at least have been an owl – which is the point of motels: you are self-sufficient and need talk to no one except when you check in and out), just before, with a sigh, I decided I might as well spend the evening catching up with some sleep, I spotted a surprising and unconvincing sign, in small letters, which said 'Restaurant'. Without hope I went the way the arrow pointed, along an unlit and of course perfectly silent passage, pushed a door and came upon a scene which, if not bouncingly lively, suggested that if there was non-domestic, non-television-watching life in New Norfolk it was here.

By an iron stove a bald man sat, sipping beer, with something of the aspect of a genial gnome. He welcomed me in Irish cadences and turned out to be from Westmeath. (His wife, surprisingly slim and pretty, considering, as she told me, she had eleven children, was English. Did nobody *Tasmanian* run anything in that country?) The gnome announced that he was the proprietor of the Amaroo Motel, and had been for seven days. I privately hoped he was not too depressed about his investment, because, to say the least, his hotel was quiet. However, he told be that previously he had run 'The Worst Pub in the World' – later I found that there was such a place, so named, in the north-east corner of the island – 'in a parish of twenty-eight souls. You couldn't commit a sin there if you tried'. I wondered how he could have made a living there, never mind commit a sin, but clearly the silences of the Amaroo would not bother him. However, he was now telling me that he had laid En Tout Cas tennis-courts all over Australia, and I lost the thread.

In the middle of the room, eating (I was relieved to see), sat a long carefully-bearded American – 'in the logging business' – wearing a tartan shirt and decorated cowboy boots, who in a gravelly baritone, seemed inclined to boast. It is not certain that he was boasting, but his affection for his own country took that form of expression. Such Americans have no sense of irony. If he had run a pub it would be called 'The Best Pub in the World'. Australians have no irony at all. You are expected to say what you mean, or they look blank. What the Australians do have is a gallows humour – as in 'The Worst Pub in the World' – and a talent, amounting to genius, for the aggressive leg-pull. Two loggers came in and soon began to eat, not talking. (I was made almost drunk by this flood of company.) The American continued: 'Back home I've trees in my yard *that* thick' – making a wide angler's gesture. He decided it was time to include the two silent loggers in his conversation: 'You cutting down too many trees over here?'

One of the loggers paused, fork before mouth, eyeing him. 'Yes.'

'Same all over.'

The loggers were silent again, then one of them said, 'Know where it all goes? Woodchippings.'

'That so? That so?'

'Know where they go? Japan. Millions of tons. They bury it under their roads in plastic bags. Under the sea.'

'Sure, sure.'

'Then, when there's no more wood left in the world, they'll have it all.'

'Funny little devils, the Japs,' put in Westmeath, musingly.

'And another thing.' The logger warmed to his task. 'D'you know they've sold the Australian War Cemetery at Gallipoli? To the Japanese? As a tourist attraction?'

'*What?*' That was from me. The information meant little to the American, who was nodding, 'Sure, sure.' (The cemetery is a national shrine.)

'Heard it on TV. Nearly fell out of my chair.'

When I got back to Launceston and told this tale I was barracked, accused of having fallen for the archetycal Australian tease, their way of keeping foreigners in their place. I had not believed what the logger was saying – it was beyond belief – but the way he said these things had suggested he believed them himself. I had not understood what great actors in this game the Australians are. He had exactly the right amount of wooden indignation at the doings of 'them'. Did the convicts tease their gaolers? They would have certainly teased each other in this slightly cruel way.

The American uncoiled himself, perhaps with some dim sense that all was not as it should be, and declared himself ready for an early night. After he went, the loggers, victors of the field, continued eating with what seemed extra satisfaction, but did not exchange so much as a wink between themselves. I had failed as an anthropologist over the beer choices, but here I felt I had noted a tribal survival-skill in operation.

The road from New Norfolk to Strathgordon, towards two vast mountain lakes, Peddar and Gordon, lies at first along the Derwent river, through a muddle of little settlements that thins out as you begin to climb towards the desolate Sawback Range. At first the innumerable varieties of eucalypt, which seem to like to stay with their own kind, offer you different sorts of forest: there are the bleached dinosaur boneyards, other forests in a reasonable state of growth and collapse, then stretches of leafy roof set on graceful white columns, like the limestone pillars of a cathedral nave. Between these is short green grass on which, anywhere else, you might be tempted to picnic.

By the side of the new-built road, among the immensely aged trees, are alarming signs warning of fire-risk, painted in segments marked from 'Low' to 'Extreme' and with a dial-hand, which this dry day was set at 'Extreme'. You climb past the trees, the view opens out, and you can see why the range is so-called: its peaks are regular and angled teeth, like those of a saw. You hit cloud, climb further, it clears a little, you stop, get out of the car, and you are in a silence and a landscape like something out of Dante; it seems to reek of sorrow, as though it has undergone some ancient disaster. An unclean mist hangs in hollows below you, like breath from a marsh. White, dead trees gesture through it, at agonised angles; as far as you can see (and it is very far), there is mist, spectral barkless trees, black saw-tooth mountains, and the only sound is the occasional tormented shriek. It was long after Patrick's time that any human being set foot here; not even the original Tasmanians ventured, or so it is believed.

All this is seen from the road the hydro-electric people have blasted through the wilderness in order to build their dams. They seem apologetic about it, and occasionally put educational labels on raw, displaced boulders: 'Ordovician' – which is the name of a tribe of ancient Britons – as though to assure us it was all done for our enlightenment, or even, at some unconscious level, as an act of propitiation to the long secrecy they have broken. But they waste their time. Even the ancient Britons feel familiar and close compared to this place.

After this Purgatory, or Hell, comes the calm Paradise of the high lakes. John Mitchel wondered why the beauties of the high Tasmanian lakes should not be 'be-rhymed', why the 'Carthaginian' Lake District should have its poets, and not these. There was a rainbow that afternoon, with the beginnings of a coloured sunset, and the smooth, island-dotted waters of Lake Pedder deserved celebration, but there would have to be a note of caution in it. It is not a natural lake any more. People I spoke to in Launceston, afterwards, lamented the white shingle beaches, the little islands, the Huon pine trees, some of them two thousand years old, now under hundreds of feet of water since the lake was flooded. Then, I did not know it was a flooded lake.

Tasmania, with its mountain torrents, lends itself to hydro-electrical engineering. At one time the islanders were besought to use as much of the stuff as possible, in order to justify these vast inundations. The argument rages: on the one hand people say: What are we destroying? Could it be the climate of our hemisphere? Others say: We need the power, we need the jobs, stop moaning. But there is doubtfulness, even among the hard-headed; everyone is shifty on the subject, even the Hydro-Electric Commission puts up notices saying, 'Please remember that all the plants and animals in the area are protected' – which is rich, coming from an organisation that has just drowned hundreds of square miles of them and is lobbying to drown more. We need the lights that lit the cheerful restaurant on Hobart docks, perhaps we even need the power that energised the television lamps that so quickly glazed the eye of the suffocated fish, but we cannot need so many or so much, when the source is such destruction. It happens far away, it is hidden, but it nags at the minds of the islanders; yet another cause for unease.

The Lake Pedder Motor Inn is as far up the road, and into the rainforest, as it is possible to go. It was a barracks for the dam-builders, who have nearly finished here, so it is partly an hotel. As soon as I checked in, it began to rain. I looked out of the window on to the inevitable carpark, watching the rain and the green rosella parrots that pecked about on the gravel, and considered it appropriate that it should rain on the rainforest, which I was determined to enter if I could; it was only a few hundred yards away. I had no raincoat and decided to wait. The rain grew heavier, torrential, and evening came on. Nothing for it but to go out and be wet. Then I remembered I had a collapsible umbrella in my bag and, amused by the absurdity, walked to the fringes of the rainforest protected by that.

Cut through a part of it was a short path called 'Jack's Track', but I hoped to scorn that and make one of my own. I had never seen a rainforest. As soon as I was confronted by the intertwined impenetrable density of it I gratefully stepped on to, or rather into, 'Jack's Track'. There was a light-green darkness inside, like the hothouse at Kew out of control; what had been cleared was about the width of a man and everything clawed and tore at the ridiculous umbrella so that I abandoned it and willingly surrendered myself to the wet (that tweed jacket had already shown signs of wilting). The rain did not fall into the forest; it hit the high canopy and bounced and rolled and splashed down from leaf to leaf. Among the trees and on the trees and from the trees, some of which had been there since Christ was in Palestine, above them, below them, so that there was only inches of space between, sprang intricate ferns, exotic grasses, laurel, myrtle, rosemary, mountain berry, all flowering, drinking, swaying, pullulating, dancing in the rain and the wet green light. It was a scene of secret exuberance and energy, even of joy, for everything had what it needed to grow and flourish in an exaggeration of abundance, for hundreds of miles, hundreds of years. After slithering and sliding for half a curved, dark mile on Jack's carefully placed planks and logs, I emerged gratefully, wet as a rat, happy to have paid even that small due to the electric force inside there. Its power, its electricity – derived from water, and light – is impossible to get out of your mind. It is indestructible. Then you remember that it can be destroyed, if given too much of what it needs, by being drowned.

Next day, in damp clothes that had assumed a curious shape, I set off for the gentle south-east.

Tasmanians are fond of saying that their climate can contain 'four seasons in a day'. Let us hope they have not changed it, by drowning too much rainforest. In a day of driving it can have as many landscapes, from British Columbia, to the *Inferno*, through Cumberland, to Sussex. The distinctions in weather and vegetation can be marked within a few miles; indeed Rex, the pilot, had said that the east part of Hobart town could be 'one overcoat warmer' than the west, because of the influence of Mount Wellington; and whereas the west coast is fierce and terrible – the first convict punishment station was there, at Macquarie Harbour, and the place proved too savage even for those implacable punishers – the east coast, on the Tasman Sea, is calm and mild.

To reach it you pass through places with Irish names, like Avoca – where John Mitchel met up with his leader, William Smith O'Brien – and English ones, like the twelve gum trees in a pasture called Epping Forest. Sometimes the cultural references are even more unlikely. One entirely isolated house, set into a hill and from which there would be no possibility of escape, advertised 'Accommodation. Fawlty Towers.'

After miles of rolling alpine pastures, lonely farms, hills like the South Downs, you climb the Elephant Pass and suddenly see scarlet pet-shop parakeets at the sides of the road and find yourself among vegetation – ferns, elaborate mosses, sawgrass – as rich and neatly kempt, by nature, as you might find lining the drive of a grand hotel on the Riviera. At the top of the pass, before you begin the descent to the Tasman Sea, slung across the road between two white and creeper-hung trees, is an enormous black silhouette of a teacup and saucer. That day, two dishevelled kookaburras had chosen to perch on top of it.

The odd thing, and an indication of the split mind a traveller learns to develop in Tasmania, is that the banality of that sign, among such luxuriant Mediterranean and sub-tropical foliage, within sight of the blue, sandy lagoons below, is not disconcerting. Perhaps the presence of the untidy-looking kookaburras helped, but it seemed emblematic of the puzzled affection the Tasmanians have for their island, why they call it 'Tassie'; it was 'Taswegian'. After all, this is a place for holidays, and a fair way from anywhere most people would be coming from, so they would be grateful for the sign and the tea it advertises. Such vast stretches of their island are horrific, or at least inhospitable, it is natural that Tasmanians should make the other parts as cosy as possible. The sign was not aimed at foreign tourists; it was there to cheer themselves.

The coast is a succession of white beaches with glass-green breakers, empty of people and houses, with fields down to the sands cropped by the usual kangaroo-like sheep. There even seem to be umbrella pines on grassy knolls, but this is not the Mediterranean: these are gum trees, 'celery-tops'. It is an unspoiled dream, unlikely ever to be spoiled because it is so far away. Occasionally a little whaler haven has been turned into a small resort; perfect, the South of France before the English found it.

It all appeared so safely remote from any danger of commercialisation. In Launceston, an acquaintance remembered Coles Bay lovingly from childhood holidays: 'You must go there, miles from anywhere. Eat a fresh crayfish sandwich on the beach.' It was at the end of a peninsula, at the end of a dirt road. Surely that would be even more safe and perfect? Perhaps it is always a mistake to accept recommendations based on the past. 'Holiday Villas. Inspect a Model One'. 'Caravan Park. Scheduled Open December 1988'. This was the cusp of change. Pink granite cliffs rose out of a warm-looking sea, there was a special kind of calm in the air; but there were no crayfish sandwiches, only a hotdog, with HP Sauce, handed over with the indifferent impatience always found in over-visited places. The aborigines had been there in numbers, which was a pleasant thought because it is, or was, a good place. Samuel Coles found their middens of oyster-shells there by the harbour, and burnt them to make lime for the building of nearby Swansea. (*Swansea?*) There are rumours that in the harbour there will be moored a huge floating hotel. On the way back, past the building-lots for holiday villas, the projected caravan park, on the dusty road lay the beautiful body of the rare, native, south-eastern oull.

It had been a long detour, and it is important if you want to try to understand a place, not to allow yourself to become tired. On the main road back to Hobart, along the sea I passed 'Shea's Crek' and 'Patterson's Bridge', surely convict names, and I remembered that as this part of the island had early been settled by convicts, it ought to be looked at. But I had experienced too many climates and landscapes, had allowed myself to be lulled into a sub-Mediterranean doze, startled awake by the taste of HP Sauce. It served me right, I thought, grimly driving back to the archive, and I passed a sight I have not been able to forget, because I did not stop. There was an unexpectedly old-looking graveyard by the side of the otherwise lonely road, and in it stood two men in dungarees, leaning on their hoes. Near the graveyard was the only wooden church I had seen on the island. The convict-built churches are all of stone but these were not primarily for the convicts. Was this a *convict* churchyard, perhaps tended by descendants? I debated turning back, but felt shy of disturbing the absorbed solitude of those two men, that picture from the cover of an old *Saturday Evening Post*. But there was another reason why I did not turn back, and thereby perhaps missed a significant clue about the early life of the island: it was too late. I pulled into the side of the road into what turned out to be a great stench, probably from a fish-meal factory, but even that could not deter me: I was immediately, irresistibly, asleep.

12

Convicts

The hurry to get back to Hobart was because Anne Rand had come up with something about convicts, and therefore something about authority.

The Irish are usually thought to have a casual attitude towards authority; perhaps because their leaders taught them for centuries to mistrust the 'foreign' authority set over them. Perhaps – it is as well to be tentative – this is what made them so notably obedient to the Church, for a man needs some sort of authority outside himself. Possibly the international nature of this allegiance has made it easier today for so many Irishmen to slot comfortably into authoritative positions in the councils of Europe, where they seem more naturally European than their British counterparts. But it is a heady business, trying to draw logical sequence from great stretches of history; safer to keep it personal.

It had slowly become clear to me that one of the reasons I was in pursuit of Patrick, perhaps the chief reason, was puzzlement at my own attitude to authority, which had annoyed everybody, except my father, and which seemed ingrained, as though inherited. The question had consciously surfaced in my confusion – nothing wrong with that: uncertainty can be a kind of freedom; clarity and logic have only a partial authority over us – when contemplating the Croppie Grave in Carlow. Patrick had fled Carlow to make a new life in the ultimate manifestation of authority, a prison. What had been his attitude to authority if mine (which I had often been taught, sometimes angrily, to identify loosely as 'Irish') derived in any way from his?

On his 1851 census form he had marked that in his household there was one 'Unfree' female. Therefore he had had a female convict servant. What had she done, and how had the Kavanaghs treated her? To find out about her might be to learn something about them. I was told that this would probably be impossible (she was not named on the form), but while I had been in the wildernesses Anne Rand had been in the archives and had traced her – had, as it turned out, traced three servants – and I was eager to hear about them.

Robert Hughes, in *The Fatal Shore*, describes the appalling punishments given to prisoners who consistently offended while on the island. But the majority cannot have done so, or not seriously. Most had gone to work for islanders; these were given conditional liberty surprisingly quickly, after a period of probation, and most of them settled on the island. It would be good to learn that this 'Female, Unfree' was one of these.

Back in Hadley's Orient Hotel Anne Rand undid her corded bales. (Hadley, who built the hotel and owned it, had come out as a convict. There is no doubt that many prospered.)

Alas, taking tea downstairs in Hadley's hotel, we learned that it was not at all sure that poor Biddy Hines, from Tipperary, profited from her Van Diemen's Land experience. Peace to her shade, but she was the first of the three unfree servants whom the Kavanaghs hired, for £8 a year, and she was a great nuisance to others and to herself.

The writing on her convict record is tiny. There is a great deal of it and it is difficult to read, but Anne Rand used her experience to transcribe it; and because it is one of authority's Van Diemen's Land biographies, from sentence to freedom, it is worth putting here in full, as it appears, leaving out only the various magistrates' initials. My interpolations are in square brackets.

Hynes Biddy   Transported for larceny. *Gaol Report*: Once convicted before. Good. [behaviour?] Married. Stated this offence: Stealing a piece of canvas from Mr Acres [?] Castle Str. Once for a sheet. 4 months. Married husband Henry at native place. 2 children. Tipperary 15 July 1844 – 7 Yrs arrived 2nd January 1845. Roman Catholic.

Trade. Farm servant. *Height* 5 1½. *Age* 30. *Complexion* Sallow. *Head* Oval. *Hair* Black. *Whiskers* –. *Visage* Oval. *Forehead* High. *Eyebrows* Brown. *Eyes* Hazel. *Nose* Sharp. *Mouth* Wide. *Chin* Large.

Marks. Pockpitted. Scar on left arm. Scar on right arm.

Station of Gang. 1st [period of detention] 15/7/45; 2nd 27/1/46; 3rd 2/6/1846.

Offences and sentences: June 19 1846, Kermode [i.e. in the service of Kermode] Disobedience of orders. *One month's hard labour*, Factory, Launceston [the female prison]. [Illegible] 3rd July 1846. 30th April 1847. Jones. Insolence. *Reprimanded.* April 12 1848 [Illegible]. Delivered of an illegitimate child 5 August 1847. Treating her child with cruelty. *Reprimanded,* June 1 1848. Disobedience of orders. *7 days added to her probation,* October 31 1848. Throwing away her child's frock, *Admonished* Dec 4 1848. James Blackburn [an architect and ex-convict]. Being on the premises of Mr Walker on the night of Sunday 3 December 1848. *48 hours cells.* June 8 1849 Palmer. Absent without leave. *14 days cells. Ticket of Leave* [if granted she could earn wages and live where she wished] *refused*; to apply in three months 13/6/49. August 1 1849 Heaps. Absent without leave, *14 days hard labour.* August 24 1849 Dowling. Larceny under £5. *12 months hard labour.* Apprehended. November 19 1849. Causing a letter to be written. *14 days cells.* Oct 22 1850 Kavanagh. Out after hours. *16 days cells.* January 8th 1851, Neglect of duty. *Three months hard labour.* Apprehended 10/1/1851. March 29 1851. Being out after hours. *One month hard labour.* April 30 1851 absent. *14 days cells.* July 1 1851 Graham. Insolence and disobedience of orders. *3 months hard labour,* Apprehended, 4/7/1851.

Free Cert [Certificate of Freedom]. 4 October 1851.

That occupies about two and a half inches of copperplate handwriting, by different clerks (presumably: the offences were committed in various places, and each clerk had a different way of recording the date and different use of punctuation), but the writing is uniform, as though by one man. The reader is almost as sorry for the clerks and the magistrates as he may be for Biddy Hines. Her punishments were clearly useless as deterrents, but her record does not suggest any special vindictiveness on the part of authority.

If she was released from penal detention on 2 June 1846, then she served only two years of a seven-year sentence (including the sea journey) in confinement. After that she went out to work and all she had to do was behave. But within seventeen days she was back in gaol, with a month's hard labour for disobedience of the orders of the Kermodes, Mr or Mrs. No need to be kind to Biddy Hines by being unkind to the Kermodes, but we cannot know whether 'Disobedience of orders' deserved a month at the washtub in the female penitentiary of Launceston, unless we know how reasonable the orders were or how great the degree of disobedience. For treating her child with cruelty she is only reprimanded: she may have been reported in some act of irritation by a busybody; she may have thrown away her child's clothes because they had been given her in a patronising fashion by some lady-bountiful and she didn't fancy the colour; and so on. You could make what stories you liked out of these copperplate facts. A pity the Kavanaghs caused her to be given sixteen days in the cells for being 'Out after hours'; but by this time there were four young children in the house (including my grandfather), one of them under five years old, and a fifth was born on 16 October, so 22 October or thereabouts was a bad time for her to stay out, from the Kavanaghs' point of view. Indeed, it is easy to picture the desperate Patrick, wife in bed, young mouths to feed, running to the magistrate to complain, so that he could at least get a replacement quickly.

That Dowling entry: presumably she stole from Henry Dowling, the agent who had brought out Patrick. Did islanders not swap stories about their domestics? In England, in the days of servants, it sometimes seems that people talked of little else.

What happened to Biddy Hines and her child (not to mention the two children left behind in Tipperary) when she had done her extra three months of hard labour after her full sentence had expired in Van Diemen's Land is, of course, not recorded; presumably it is written into the subsequent history of Tasmania, which some describe as one of the most law-abiding places in the world.

There is a blank on her record where the ship's surgeon should have made his report, but on that of the Kavanaghs' next servant, Ellen O'Brien, fifty-five years old, from County Kerry, the surgeon's report is 'Artful and very deceitful'. The Kavanaghs do not appear to have been good at choosing. She was convicted at the Surrey Assizes in 1845, probably one of the many poor Irish who had settled in or near London at the time of the Famine. A widow, three times imprisoned before, for theft, assault and drunkenness. (For that she was fined 5 shillings which makes two imprisonments, not three; the records do not always make clear sense. On this one is marked no length of sentence: this sometimes happened, and convicts found themselves serving indefinite sentences because of bureaucratic muddle. Perhaps she could not afford the fine and was imprisoned instead.) Ellen O'Brien's record is similar to Biddy Hines's. She went absent immediately after being released from detention in 1846, received sentences of hard labour for drunkenness, 'For destroying a woolcard', 'for having a man on the premises for unlawful purposes'. At least the Kavanaghs laid no charge against her, and she was given her freedom in 1851.

The third and last servant of the Kavanaghs who is recorded, and probably the one mentioned on the census form, was Jane McClaren of Perth, fifty-three, sentenced to seven years' transportation in Edinburgh in 1848 for the theft of a gown. Her husband there was called Duncan. 'Surgeon's Report: Very well behaved. Remarks. Child Duncan died at Nursery, 9 September 1848.' His death took place five weeks after their arrival on the island. No mention of his age, or why he died; only the careful bureaucratic note, 'Vide Return for Sept 9 1848'. After so long a voyage, the two of them together to lose him so quickly, in the Nursery for the children of convict women. . . .

Under 'Offences and Sentences', where the records of Biddy Hines and Ellen O'Brien contain line after crabbed line, on that of Jane McClaren there is nothing written at all. It would be pleasant to think that she stayed on with the Kavanaghs, if that was a pleasant thing to do. They certainly hired no other convict servant. But on the bottom of her blank record, in faint ink, can just be read: 'T of L, 21/9/52 revoked 5/4/53.' If it means her Ticket of Leave was withdrawn, that sounds like tragedy, and there is no mention of why. This worried us. Mrs Rand investigated further and discovered that the Comptroller-General of Convicts, J. S. Hampton, the notorious defender of the Norfolk Island sadist Captain Price, Hampton, the man who drove John Mitchel's dreamy leader, William Smith O'Brien, to wish for death; who ended, in Robert Hughes's words, as 'the odious and corrupt' Governor of Western Australia – revoked all the Tickets of Leave of those who had not gone through the technicality of reporting to their District Police Office. It was a piece of bureaucratic bullying, or possibly an official muddle, for the *Launceston Examiner* of 5 April 1853 prints an immense list of those whose Tickets had been revoked, consisting entirely of women, Jane McClaren among them. There are about 150 names on that list alone, so clearly they were not all absconders; either these women had not been told to report, or it was a newly enforced regulation which before had been left in abeyance. Perhaps if she wanted to stay with the Kavanaghs the freedom of a Ticket of Leave was unnecessary to her, but all those who had not reported lost theirs for a year. It is an example of unnecessary harrying, even of those who had earned probation. These records represent more than they can say, or we can imagine, of such bureaucratic bullying and pettiness.

They do, though, help the imagination a little in respect of the Kavanagh household. It was not wealthy, nor was it at the bottom of the pile, and their choice of convict help was, on the whole, unfortunate. By 1850–1, the years when these women were hired, in addition to Mary Ann, who had come out with them, six children had been born, of whom four survived, all under ten years old: Terence, 1842?; Henry Paul (my grandfather), 1843?; Richard, 1845 (died 1846); Charles, 1846; Ellen, 1848 (died 1848); and Maria, 1850. Then came Catherine, 1853 (died); Francis, 1856; and John, 1857. Patrick and Margaret ended with a quiverful: all of them, after 1845, passing through the baptising hands of Father Thomas Butler of St Joseph's, Launceston.

In order to learn something of their circle, I had asked Mrs Rand to look for records of these children's godparents, the Fergusons, the Mahoneys, the Monaghans, the Fields, the Keoghs. That most of the names sounded Irish and to discover that they had all arrived as free settlers was not surprising; but little of interest emerged about them.

What else? In 1853 Patrick had bought a house on Brisbane Street, so by then he at least had a little money; in November 1866 he owned two houses on the street (with rateable values of £10 and £20), renting one to Benjamin Smith and the other to Charles Worlock, meanwhile living in a larger house (rateable value £60) belonging to a Mrs Yates. Can anything be made of these dry bones?

Perhaps a little, or things can be inferred. Mrs Yates was the widow of James Yates, who in 1852 was a constable at the Launceston Male House of Correction, supervisor of the treadmill there. Some time after that he became a baker and a grocer in the house on Brisbane Street, dying in 1857, and perhaps, when Patrick rented the house after his death, was the inspiration that made him style himself 'baker', a trade there was no mention of before or after.

Perhaps Mrs Yates no longer lived in the house; perhaps her husband's job of treadmill supervisor, punisher, bore no taint equivalent to that of flagellator; perhaps it was a straight transaction, simply the renting of a vacant house, and Patrick had no contact with the Yateses at all. Nevertheless – clutching at straws for evidence – I found here a suggestion that he had some contact, in business terms anyway, with the operators of the penal system. Probably it was impossible not to have such contact.

In this respect the renting of one of his houses to Charles Worlock is of interest, because Worlock had been a convict, 'twice transported', a Port Arthur man. 'There is something so lowering', remarked the Lieutenant-Governor, Sir John Franklin, 'attched to the name of a Port Arthur Man.' It was the place of harshest punishment, on the Tasman Peninsula.

Worlock had been transported from Bristol for seven years, convicted of larceny, and arrived in 1842. He was a shoemaker by trade, and in 1846 was given two months' hard labour for making five pairs of boots 'on his own account without permission'. In all the convict records there are signs of a bureaucratic system of punishment that is without light. To make shoes is precisely what he should have been encouraged to do, especially in an island as short of useful skills as Van Diemen's Land. At all events, within a year of that punishment, in 1847, he was given his Ticket of Leave, and seems to have lived quietly enough for eight years. Then, as so often happened on that island of punishments whose only possible excuse could be that they deterred, he offended again, in a serious way.

In 1855 he stole £1 and a till from one Titus Brown, but he

was carrying a weapon: it was 'Robbery under Arms'. For this he was, in the confusing terms of 'the system', 'Again Transported', this time for twenty years, to Port Arthur, where life for recidivists was made as nearly unendurable as possible. Even visiting administrators, who were supposed to have authorised such things, confessed themselves shamed to see convicts yoked to rail-trucks, pulling them uphill. Working on this railroad, tied to a truck and three years into his sentence, Worlock was sentenced, for 'Insolence', to '7 Days Solitary Cell'. The cell is still there, lightless, soundless. Even in the merciless regime of Port Arthur prisoners were allowed a day off work after even a short period inside it, so disoriented did they emerge. That charge of insolence could well have been brought by an overseer who was himself a convict. One of the most terrible aspects of the System, as it was called, is that the 'officer class' barely sullied themselves by day-to-day contact with the prisoners, but handed them over to convict overseers who could indulge what spite or sadism they chose.

But the System had its mercies or, more possibly, its economies. After only four years of his twenty-year sentence Worlock was given his Ticket of Leave, a conditional pardon in 1861 and a free pardon in 1867. This would have allowed him to return home to Bristol if he could afford it, but he did not; he had rented Patrick's house in Brisbane Street. There, with his ex-convict wife, he set up as a shoemaker – which is clearly what he had wanted to do from the outset. (His wife's charge-sheet contains examples of the varying literacy of clerks. She had been charged with stealing 'a ridicule' – reticule? – and the surgeon's report describes her as being 'Quiet, passionate and quarrelsome'.)

All this was not much straw to clutch, but it did at least suggest a cheerful disinterestedness on the part of Patrick, living in the house of the widow of the treadmill supervisor, and renting his own house to an ex-highwayman.

But perhaps by the time Worlock moved in Patrick had left

the island. He made over both his houses to his second son, Henry Paul, my grandfather, who must have been about twenty-three at this time, 1866. Henry Paul, for some reason, promptly mortgaged them, confusingly giving right of attorney to James Kavanagh, who was no relation as far as I know. Perhaps he did this to raise money for the family fare to New Zealand, but it seems odd that he did not sell. (On the documents of the transaction Henry Paul described himself as 'cabinet maker', but when he next appears in the records, in New Zealand, he is a 'farmer'. Perhaps he was following the example of his inventive father, but the 'cabinet maker' claim is intriguing because he ended up as Chief Surveyor of Forests, whereas from 'groom' to 'baker' is too big a jump; at least Henry Paul maintained an interest in wood.)

On the baptismal register of St Joseph's, Launceston, in 1856, there appears a name, standing as godfather to baby Francis, of particular significance to the Kavanaghs: that of Father James Paul. Margaret's brother, of an age with Patrick, Archbishop Cullen's nephew, he was part of Cullen's network of relations and friends sent to Catholicise the Antipodes. There is no record of his arrival in the island: perhaps he was godparent in name only, but it would fit because in that year he was on his way to New Zealand. Ten years later, in 1866, well established as parish priest at Onehunga, outside Auckland, he appears to have suggested that his sister and her family come there to join him. Anyway, that is what they did.

There is no record of their leaving Tasmania, Patrick and Margaret and Mary Ann nearly a quarter of a century on the island, and the seven younger ones born there. They must have made the week-long journey travelling steerage, which suggests either poverty or prudence; probably the latter, but they cannot be said to have left in triumph to begin their new chapter.

I tried to squeeze more juice from these convict documents before I followed Patrick's family to Auckland. It was clear, for instance, that pardoned convicts did not often return home, so the island cannot have been too bad a place. Perhaps they could not afford to travel, but there is plenty of evidence that free life in Van Diemen's Land was preferable to any life most of them could have found in England, or in Ireland. This was one reason for the ascending scale of punishments: it had to be a place whose name was dreaded in England, not an attractive one, so the authorities coolly made it dreadful. For those who continued to reoffend the punishments became so ferocious that you begin to believe authority has gone mad. Perhaps it did for a time, because of its own mad logic: that the more you punished a man the more likely you were to bring him to his senses. Many prisoners died, preferred to die, rather than give in to this, and it is hard not to believe that these, in luckier circumstances, would have been valuable men.

Some prisoners, of course, 'co-operated'; with its final degradation, 'dobbing', informing on their fellows. That was how the System was run. The famous bushranger Martin Cash was possibly one of those, at last brought to heel by the System. He spent time at Port Arthur, and even longer on the final hell-hole, Norfolk Island; he lived to tell the tale, to describe both places. To read his descriptions is to become unable to forget them.

We sat there in comfort in Hadley's Orient Hotel, Anne Rand and I: the attentive young man, once of the Groucho Club, bringing us tea as we scanned these bare records of unknown dead people, records of their suffering, their lack of luck. It was too comfortable. Port Arthur had to be visited; it was one of the few remnants of the System allowed to remain standing in Tasmania, and had been the worst.

13

Port Arthur

It would have been good to be able to arrive at the prison peninsula by sea, past Storm Bay and through the basalt cliffs that guarded Port Arthur. But 'Cap'n Bob' would not oblige, and there is now a road from Hobart, a journey of about sixty miles through the Forestier Peninsula and across a narrow strip like a causeway, Eagle Hawk Neck, which joins the Tasman Peninsula tenuously to the main island. On one side of the Neck is the open sea; on the other side, on this day, a comparatively calm stretch of water sheltered on both shores by inhospitable scrub. It was across this that Cash and Jones and Kavanagh swam when they made their celebrated escape in 1843, going on to terrorise the island, including Launceston, during the first years that Patrick and Margaret were settling there. The three arrived on the other side naked; their clothes, tied to their heads, had been swept off by a wave. Each thought the others had drowned, and when they came upon each other 'in a state of nature' they sat down and laughed. Cash dictated an account of this swim, and their further adventures, when he was an old man, and though he makes much of this devil-may-care side of the business there was undoubtedly something of that in his nature.

They had to be brave to swim across because they believed the water was full of sharks; it was put about among the prisoners that guards threw offal in the water to attract them, and perhaps they did. Across the narrow neck nine dogs were chained on leashes sufficiently long for no space to be left between them, yet not so long that they could eat each other, only convicts. In front of these dogs, at night, was set a row of oil lamps upon a line of crushed white shells. With reason the Commandant believed it nearly impossible to escape, and even if anyone did, in that landscape, it must have been nearly impossible to survive.

The prison was set up in 1832 by Governor Arthur as a place for second or persistent offenders and his Standing Instructions make its purpose clear: 'The most unceasing labour is to be exacted from the convicts, and the most harassing vigilance is to be observed.' Thomas Lemprière, the Commissary Officer, by no means a monster, thought the description 'an earthly Hell' exaggerated; when amended to 'abode of misery', he pondered the phrase and wrote, 'to that cognomen we do not object.' That, he added, was what Port Arthur was intended to be.

Arthur's problems (among many; at this time he was also trying to round up the aborigines) were the exhortations from London to make the island more dreaded; word was getting about that Van Diemen's Land was in some ways preferable to England, and to Ireland, because at least somebody there had responsibility to see that you ate. Perhaps its regime was not sadistic by the standards of the time, but by 1847 a Governor who succeeded Arthur, Sir William Denison, was unsure about this: 'I must say that my feelings at seeing myself seated, and pushed along by these miserable convicts, were not very pleasant. It was painful to see them in the condition of slaves, which, in fact, they are, waiting for me up to their knees in water.' He does not mention, perhaps he did not know, that under the water, below their knees, the slaves wore chains. He is talking of the convict-drawn railway where Charles Worlock, shoemaker and highwayman, was given seven days in the Silent Cell for Insolence.

The regime was not haphazardly cruel, with the important exception of its most pernicious defect, unquestioning reliance on the reports of convict overseers. There was a worse place, Norfolk Island, a thousand miles away in the middle of the ocean, where the Commandants were more or less given their heads, too far away to be controlled; at least one of these, the infamous Captain Rose Price, turned it into something reminiscent of medieval paintings of the tortures of the damned. When Bishop Willson, who had so much trouble getting his cathedral built in Launceston, visited Norfolk Island, he was so horrified that he turned round and sailed back to England to report what he had seen to the House of Lords. This caused such an impression that conditions improved on Norfolk, for a time. (Hampton, the 'Comptroller' who revoked Jane McClaren's Ticket of Leave, counter-reported that Willson was exaggerating.)

Almost the strangest thing about Port Arthur, in view of what went on there, is that pictorially it is an idyll and must always have been so. The convicts were surely surprised, when they passed through the high cliffs as though entering the ultimate natural dungeon, to find themselves in a green dell. Today, along the road, the passage is through a banality of bungalows but the surprise is almost as great. You end at a small lapping harbour, a penitentiary in pretty pink brick, originally built as a granary and still looking like one. In the centre of the open park-like space, surrounded by wooded hills, is a large village green, a mower moving up and down it as at Lord's, with avenues of chestnuts around it, a large church to one side, and the elegant cottages of the settlement officers. They do in fact play cricket on that green; on this day it was being scampered across by coach parties of schoolchildren.

From this English green comes the inevitable Tasmanian shock: chestnut-tree-surrounded, it is dotted with English plovers, lapwings, in England sometimes called peewits because of their pleasant call, but when these rise and fly off it is with harsh, croaking screams like the souls of flogged convicts.

The chestnuts are imported; so are the oak trees round the Commandant's house, filled with Grass-Green parrots which have adapted and now feed on acorns. His house adapted itself

itself too. In 1877, when the settlement was abandoned, it became the Carnavon Hotel, so spelled. The rest of the place the authorities invited the islanders to dismantle, as though to remove the memory of it. The first drunken tourists accidentally burned some of it down. Then, like the Cities of the Plain, it was struck by thunderbolts, more than once, and gutted by bushfires. It is a tribute to convict building that so much of it still stands. It lingered on as a prison for twenty-five years after the end of transportation because it contained convicts who had been there so long they had nowhere else to go – 'the Old Crawlers'. Sometimes these put balls and chains on themselves to earn pennies from tourists. Most of them had gone mad: 111 of them were certified to be mad (still the crabbed, clerkly hand writes its careful record) and these outnumbered the ones who had managed to stay sane. The remaining prison buildings ended up, as perhaps they were always bound to do, asylums.

The Cities of the Plain analogy is exact. That old granary contained separate cells, 136 of them, but its upper floors were enormous dormitories and these held *513 men*. Even the most sympathetic observers were appalled by the brutalising effect of the system on some of the prisoners in Port Arthur; it would have been these who held sway over the dormitories. It was news of 'irregularities', of 'abominations', reaching London, that most alarmed the government, especially the Secretary for the Colonies, William Gladstone. The worst horror for a convict, in any prison, must be his fellow prisoners.

Perhaps to prevent these things an even madder place was built, in 1848: 'the Model Prison', on the design of Pentonville. Fifty cells for silent solitary confinement in which prisoners were intended to sit and contemplate the error of their ways. They were not allowed to talk, and so that there should be no sound at all the warders wore felt over their shoes. The inmate had no name, only a number, and had to wear a mask whenever he left his cell. A horrible, soft-peaked cap was devised; it had to be pulled over the face, and contained two little eye-slits. They had always to remain five yards apart when in single file, and were forbidden, on pain of extra punishment, even to pause outside the shut door of another cell. Those cells, and the tiny individual exercise yards, high-walled, shaped like pieces of cheese, still stand. So does the Silent Cell, a silence within a silence, and entirely dark. It was planned that all prisoners, for the good of their souls, should spend some part of their sentence in this 'Model Prison', but it is recorded, with what sounds like surprise, that it so deranged those confined in it that it came to be used as a place of punishment for the worst offenders.

The Tasmanian myth of Van Diemen's Land is in many ways correct. It is part of the terrible logic of the System that you could indeed be transported for the theft of a gown, offend again and go down a rung in the System until you were caught on a down-escalator of retribution and could find yourself flogged nearly to death, in chains or in the Silent Cell at Port Arthur. This undoubtedly happened to some who could barely understand the sequence.

The more you think about the System and about the whole idea of transportation, the more you are driven to the view that it was only made possible by a lunatic, fundamentally un-christian, concept of class. Perhaps it is the final banishment of this class idea, at least from Australia, that is the best, unwished-for, outcome of transportation.

The representatives of authority on the island never seemed to question what they were doing; as they surely would have done if they had thought the convicts were men like themselves. They were there to make the System work; it was the concern of some to make the System work as justly as possible; but the idea that there could be any way, other than violent physical punishment, of dealing with working-class offenders, if it ever entered the heads of most of them, went in and out, in Martin

Cash's phrase, 'like sunshine'. The working class, if not a different species altogether, were recalcitrant children, to be punished like children, but with punishments commensurate with their adulthood and more than commensurate.

No 'gentleman' was flogged, or treated as the working-class prisoners were, or not without extraordinary dismay, as though a natural order was being threatened. Throughout the history of transportation prisoners who were not working class were thought of as aberrations and were certainly an embarrassment. Of course, they might have friends, connections in high places; but it went deeper than that. It was as though, buried below consciousness, never articulated, inside the assumptions of the age, there was a knowledge that flogging, as well as doing physical injury, was a psychic outrage that destroyed something in a man. To see a 'gentlemen' so broken, so humiliated, would make the edifice of authority based on social hierarchy totter. That was too dangerous.

We see this social unease in the treatment of Mitchel, not only because he was a political prisoner; he was also a gentleman. His leader, William Smith O'Brien, was given his own private cottage in Port Arthur; it is still there, a place of Irish pilgrimage. Sentenced to death for leading the fiasco of the rising in 1848, his sentence commuted to transportation for life, O'Brien was at first confined on Maria Island, where his host was the dreaded Hampton. So sure was O'Brien that Hampton was not treating him according to rank that he complained to London and was removed to the cottage in Port Arthur. But even he, a gentle man (wholly, one would have thought, unsuited to insurrection), seems to have given little thought to what was going on around his cottage, or at least not radically to have questioned it. As for John Mitchel, we have seen that he thought his fellow convicts less than human.

Stories of extraordinary punishment abound and are recorded elsewhere. Let one stand for all: from a tale told by Martin Cash, and not about himself.

In his memoirs, dictated in old age, Cash describes himself as coming from a well-to-do family in Wexford – did any Irishman ever confess himself descended from peasants? – transported at the age of eighteen for trying to shoot a friend who had stolen his girl, a *crime passionnel*. After many years cattle-ranging on the mainland of Australia, soon given his Ticket of Leave, he again fell into trouble (never his fault, we are to understand, always a result of his open and trusting nature) and eventually found himself at Port Arthur, 'where I had no intention of staying'. From there he made the famous escape, with Kavanagh, a fellow Irishman, and Jones, a Londoner (in his account he never divulges their christian names).

After that they ranged the bush for a couple of years, holding up private and public houses, usually with theatrical gallantry towards the ladies on Cash's part (which was what probably saved his neck) until he was caught in Hobart on his way, oddly enough, to shoot a man who had made off with his 'companion' (as he always calls her). He admits that he intended to shoot her too. In the course of his arrest he killed a constable. His death sentence was commuted on a technicality, which caused indignation (his 'gallantry' was remembered in his favour), and he was sent to the final place of punishment, Norfolk Island, for ever. There he again encountered Captain Price, to whom he had said, years before, according to himself, 'Hell would be empty without you!' Here is one of his stories about that place, an old lag's story certainly, but the instrument he describes was known to have been invented and used by Price, and somehow the last phrase has a tang of Irishness about it, beyond the invention of the formal style of the journalist who wrote his memoirs down; it gives the story an extra authenticity, but in any case there is no reason to doubt it. He begins by mentioning the visit of Bishop Willson.

Six months after the occurrences stated in the last chapter I was reinstated in my former billet, and the next vessel that arrived brought Bishop Willson who, on his tour of inspection through the establishment, entered one of the wards in the barrack-yard where he found thirty prisoners, all of whom had been recently flogged. His Lordship was nearly overpowered by the stench arising from their festering wounds and was so horrified at the spectacle that he discontinued his visits and returned to Van Diemen's Land in the vessel which brought him down. When in England he told his terrible story to the Secretary of State for the Colonies, and the result was that the benevolent interference of this truly holy and good man had the effect of decreasing the pitching of the triangle and the blood-pouring strokes of the lash.

A prisoner named Alexander Campbell had been sentenced to thirty days solitary confinement for insolence to his overseer, and while undergoing this sentence he was visited by the Commandant [Price], and being of a violent temperament he happened to make use of some 'threatening language', for which at the expiration of his term of imprisonment he was sentenced to a like term of confinement.

About this time a new instrument of torture had just been invented, in the shape of an iron frame about six feet long and two-and-a-half wide, with round iron bars placed transversely about twelve inches apart, the prisoner being placed in a horizontal position upon this frame with his head projecting over the end and without any support, was then firmly lashed with cords and in this awful agony he was left in darkness for twelve hours. Campbell was subjected to this punishment so often and for such a length of time that at last he was found dead on the stretcher when the gaoler visited his cell. From the time Campbell was first sentenced until his murder, a period of six months, he had not been altogether twelve days out of solitary confinement. As there was no person to investigate the matter, the sacrifice of Campbell passed like sunshine.

It could have occurred to authority, even in 1850, that on the truly defiant, the torture-maddened, a steady increase in punishment could result in murder. Some of its victims would indeed be mad; or simple-minded, which makes it worse.

There were those the System did 'break', of course. Possibly Cash was one, since he is thought at last to have been guilty of 'dobbing' or informing. Peter MacFee, the resident historian at Port Arthur, suspects him of this and said that, still, because of penal times, Australians regard this as the final sin. Mateship, he said, the practice of never 'dobbing' to authority, is now part of the national character; at least high in its scale of values.

At last Sir William Denison shut Norfolk Island down altogether, after rebuking Price. Cash lived to tell the tale, in his suburban orchard, a free man. Jones, the most violent of the trio, was hanged early on. Kavanagh, for alleged participation in a riot, from which Cash had wisely separated himself, was hanged on Norfolk Island. A few years later in Melbourne, Price strolled over to talk to a gang of prisoners working in a quarry. Silently they surrounded him, and beat him to death.

In 1850 William Smith O'Brien was in ill health and his fellow Young Irelanders at last talked him into accepting his Ticket of Leave. He could now leave his cottage at Port Arthur and live more or less as a free man, confined to a specified district. Finally pardoned in 1854, he returned to Ireland, 'to the bosom', as Robert Kee puts it, 'of his embarrassed family.' Kee is a sympathetic commentator, but that is not quite fair. The 'rising' O'Brien had led in 1848 (he said himself that it deserved no such name) had almost been a joke, so complete was its failure. But O'Brien belongs to the very short list of revolutionaries who are willing to die for their country but unwilling to instruct others to do so. He was of the ancient O'Briens but, an Irish colleague sneered, 'There is more Smith about him than O'Brien.' Perhaps there was; names are odd things. It is Mitchel's name that figures in the rebel songs, but, in the midst of a people starving while ships left Ireland for England loaded with food, it was O'Brien who saw that he could not wait, who took action knowing it was inopportune, that it would cost him his life. He remained consistent. Sentenced to be hanged, drawn and quartered, according to the old formula, he refused to ask for reprieve, the only way his ancient sentence could be commuted, so an embarrassed government had to pass a special Act to prevent the execution. In Van Diemen's Land he was the only Young Irelander who would not accept a Ticket of Leave and so, as a not even partially pardoned convict, he fell into the hands of Hampton on Maria Island, friend and protector of Price, whose treatment nearly killed him, and his objection to this was its illegality. From there he wrote to his subordinate Mitchel, who notes in his *Journal*: 'Even if we had the opportunity of talking together face to face, we should be sure to differ widely. He cannot endure my root-and-branch revolutionism, nor I his moderation.'

In Ireland O'Brien's hopes for a rising had been dashed by peasant memories of the reprisals after 1798, and also frustrated by the priests, who told their parishioners not to follow him. When O'Brien and Mitchel at last met on the island he spoke of this and Mitchel could barely contain his disgust: '(what shall I call it? – the cowardice, the treachery, or the mere priestliness) of the priests . . . when the people seemed to be gathering in force, they came whispering round, and melted off the crowds like silent thaw.'

The idea of 'Irishness' is often connected with Romanism, and with disaffection abetted by the priesthood. One of the many confusing strands in it is that some of the most influential figures in Irish history (and romance), like John Mitchel, could stand neither priests nor the Church. Now the story of Mitchel was to take a turn that twists the strand even further.

An Irish gunman arrives in Van Diemen's Land, P.J. Smyth, nicknamed 'Nicaragua' because of his revolutionary activities in South America. He has been sent from the United States to assist in the escape of Mitchel and O'Brien. But first – insists the Old World O'Brien – as men of honour they must surrender their Tickets of Leave in their two districts, an action which would obviously arouse suspicion. 'If opposed,' notes Mitchel, 'then any sort of violence (O'Brien says, short of killing) shall be allowable.' It is impossible not to like O'Brien. Mitchel takes no notice, goes to his magistrate secretly armed, with the armed 'Nicaragua' at his side, resolved to shoot the magistrate (whom he knows and from whom he bought the horse on which he hopes to ride away) and to shoot the innocent constable also, should there be any difficulty. 'A great man is Mr Colt – one of the greatest minds in our country,' says Smyth. Mitchel wrote that down, with apparent approval.

They do not need to shoot the magistrate, who is suspicious but hesitant, and while he hesitates Mitchel jumps on the horse and escapes from custody, though not yet from the island. There follows a series of frustrations in his attempts to get off it: rescue ships turning up at the wrong place, or not at all, weeks of soakings and hardships, of disguises and dangers; genuinely exciting and brave, and they would make a good film. At last he does get off the island, to Melbourne, to Tahiti, and thence to California where, predictably, he is given a hero's welcome.

The man who helps him escape at last, from Launceston, when all others have failed, who hides him in his church, who disguises him in his soutane, is Patrick and Margaret's friend and priest, Father Butler, baptiser of their children.

In the meantime the good Father Butler proposes to conceal me in the belfry of his church. How can I ever acknowledge the great services rendered to me by all these kind people?

The Rev. Mr Blake [Mitchel] has accomplished his perilous journey. The night-coach started from Launceston at half-past-five p.m., when there is still daylight; and Father Butler would by no means hear of my going to the coach office in the most public part of town. He therefore lent me a horse, and rode with me out of town, to wait for the coach at Frankland Village. As we rode on we approached a turnpike gate. 'Here,' said Father Butler, 'you can test your disguise. Clergymen, of all denominations, are privileged to pass the toll-gates free in Van Diemen's Land. If the man has no doubt of you being a priest, he will politely touch his hat to us both. But if he does not believe in your holy orders, it will cost you threepence.' [One wonders what it would have cost Father Butler.] I saved the three-pence, and my dignified nod was as good as a blessing to the gatekeeper.

(The cowardice, the treachery, the mere priestliness of the priests . . .)

Some will think that Father Butler should not have done this: Mitchel was the most wanted man in the colonies. More, perhaps, will find it hard to understand that as soon as I read of it I knew I had at last arrived at a point I recognised, and instinctively understood.

I did not even like Mitchel, but I knew why Father Butler helped him. He did more: he helped another Young Irelander, Terence Bellew McManus, hiding him in his presbytery and, when the police came for him, substituting a parishioner who looked like him so that they arrested the wrong man. This, remember, was a widely respected clergyman, described a century and a half later by Geoffrey Stillwell as a 'careful priest', Dean Butler, who refused a bishopric even though the Pope urged him to accept. Perhaps he did not wish for that kind of authority.

He was not only a respected priest, he was a good one. At his first Mass in Launceston in 1845 ten people took communion;

within twelve months there were sometimes two hundred. He founded the school in the little town on the convict island at which my grandfather later proved he had been taught well. Butler and Patrick knew each other; they could not have avoided doing so if they had tried. The Catholic community was small, a fifth of the perhaps ten thousand inhabitants of Launceston. Apart from the baptisms (and the burials) and the membership of the tiny 'Rosary Circle' which Patrick and Margaret joined in 1847, they came from the same part of Ireland (Butler was from Kilkenny, the neighbour town to Carlow), and there were also Margaret's widespread clerical connections, all of whom Butler would have heard about or known. It cannot be shown that Patrick knew of Mitchel and McManus, but the way Butler behaved towards them would have been a part of the air he breathed, an air from Carlow heavy with history and now charged with news of the Famine; the air I had been trying to scent since I arrived on the island. It must have nourished the cast of mind Patrick took with him to New Zealand, and it must have been strong nourishment, because from Tasmania and New Zealand, through my grandfather and father, it seems to have come to me.

About this time, in London, Hector Berlioz attended a concert given by 6500 Charity Children in St Paul's Cathedral. He found it so moving that he says he had to use his music-sheet, 'as Agamemnon his toga, to veil my face'. What reduced him to tears was not only the music but the orderly obedience of that vast number of children. 'A great nation, which possesses the instinct of great things! The soul of Shakespeare lives in it!'

Shakespeare expresses a part of the practical, pragmatic soul of England when he has (Celtic) Glendower boast, 'I can call spirits from the vasty deep!', and (Norman) Hotspur reply: 'Why, so can I, and so can any man. But will they come when you do call for them?' Clearly Father Butler did not believe in the same spirits (or spirit) that the British authorities put their faith in, and he had a different interpretation of justice and of obedience.

Traditionally the Irish are thought to believe in many things, from miraculous statues to their own view of history. (Even Catholic historians admit that Cardinal Moran, Archbishop of Sydney, gave an account of the early days of the Church in Australia that is in some respects 'pure fiction'.) The Irish are adept at mythologising what they love, and also what they hate. It is as though the two life-views are temperamentally opposed, the Irish and the English, and it would be absurd to generalise in this way if history did not seem to bear this out. If only the two could mingle, and draw what is best from each: the Irish be less emotionally inventive, the English more receptive. It is no wonder that the two views can switch back and forth in an Anglicised Irish mind like mine, as at the Croppie Grave, and sometimes take the form of a joust, Authority versus Imagination. But I knew I had understood Father Butler.

14

Auckland

If that, possibly, was the nationalist atmosphere breathed by the man from Carlow in Van Diemen's Land, however unaffected by it he may or may not have been, what was the atmosphere he and his family would have found in New Zealand in 1866? From what there is to learn about the state of 'Irishness' in New Zealand at that time, they were about to endure hyper-ventilation. The New Zealand historian, H. R. Jackson, describes the extent of it:

> To assist in drawing a line between Catholic and Protestant the Catholic bishops had much to say about Ireland. Their reasoning was simple: the church at home was identified with the national cause; therefore to heighten consciousness of being Irish would heighten consciousness of being Catholic. Partly towards this end, it may be supposed, the Catholic cathedral in Melbourne was named after the patron saint of Ireland. In front of the cathedral was placed a statue of Daniel O'Connell, the 'Irish Liberator'. In 1875 James Quinn, Catholic bishop of Brisbane, changed his name to O'Quinn to mark the centenary of O'Connell's birth. Catholics who had never seen Ireland sang in 'Hail, Glorious St Patrick' of how their hearts burned for God, St Patrick and the land of shamrocks. The Australian Plenary Council of 1885 arranged for the celebration of the feasts of Irish saints: Fursey, Fintan, Cataldus, Frigidian, Rumbert, Kilian, Fiacre, Canice, Gall, Fridolin, Malachy, Livinus,

Lawrence O'Toole, Columbanus, Virgilius, Brendan, Bridget, and Ita. Later, Carthage and Kieran were added to the list. When Henry William Cleary was consecrated (in Ireland) bishop of Auckland the invitations were in Gaelic and Cleary ensured that his episcopal robes were made in Ireland. Norman Thomas Gilroy, who was Australian-born, arranged his episcopal consecration for 17 March, the feast of St Patrick. Strings of churches were named after Irish saints. Instances of how variations were played on this theme of Catholic Ireland could easily be multiplied, for bishops and priests never tired of it. Even Roger Vaughan, an Englishman, boosted Irishness and linked it with zeal for religion, though in his case desire to make himself acceptable to his Irish people was undoubtedly also an element. He told a friend in 1877 that he had written more in favour of the Irish people than all the Irish bishops in Australia put together. That reinforcing Catholic with Irish identity had become settled policy amongst the bishops as early as 1870 is suggested by a pastoral letter by Thomas Croke. Writing from Rome prior to taking up his appointment to the see of Auckland, Croke promised his people that he would often talk to them about Ireland, of its hopes and fears, of the wonders it has already achieved, and of all [it] is actually doing for the faith of Christ. A lively young French nun who observed Croke in action in Auckland, summed up his message as 'the faith of Ireland and the Gospel of Erin'.

The cathedral in Auckland was called after St Patrick too. From Ireland, Archbishop Cullen was at work: through his placemen, through his nephews. Father James Paul was one of his nephews and the Kavanaghs were staying with him. Over their heads the dangerous connection was being made between Catholicism and Irish nationalism, which could amount, at a safe Antipodean distance, almost to an identification of

Catholicism with disaffection. An indication of how unpopular this made the Irish, and also of the way post-Reformation bogies still haunted the English–Scottish imagination, lies in the names given to the two types of invasive scrub found in New Zealand most detested by the farmers: one was immediately dubbed 'Spaniard', the other 'Wild Irishman'.

Here, as in America, the matter could safely be made much less complex and subtle than it really was. In Ireland all sorts of ambiguities and neighbourlinesses and reasonable compromises had made it possible for Catholic and Protestant to live together, given a chance. Even after the rising in 1798 they had settled down together remarkably quickly. There, it was the interventions and anxieties of the government in London that exacerbated division, its nervousness about revolutionary infection from France.

But overseas, the need of the expatriate Irish for dignity and identity, channelled by the Church, simplified the Irish situation to the point of travesty. There is obviously much that is comic in Jackson's account but – best to admit it at once – there is a thrill in it also, for me, because it was within the echoes of that sort of noise that I was brought up. There is also some historical and contemporary truth in it. In respect of religion Ireland was, and still is, a special place. You can put it down to what you like, to the weather, to the tricks of Atlantic light, to emptiness and poverty, but Ireland gives every visitor the shock of being in a genuinely Christian country. It most probably is something to do with the light, which, when you look out at the islands in the west, makes it not at all surprising that they have been littered with holy, withdrawn men (who then went out and helped Christianise Europe), for these islands are not misty, or not for long; they have unusually clear outlines, though the outline, because of the movement of light, does not appear constant. It is a mystical, not a pragmatic, light.

A small example of the difference of atmosphere in Ireland,

taken at random; such things happen all the time: in a pub in Trim, in Westmeath, a simple-minded young man – a simpleton – is talking to the barmaid. It is early in the morning of All Saints' Day 1988. The place is empty except for the three of us, and he makes the occasional, over-loud, friendly remark towards her, while she busies herself with her tasks behind the bar, her back to him. 'Will I see you at the twelve-thirty?' he calls, meaning the mass at that time. 'No', she says, fixing an optic, 'I went last night.' 'There is a twelve-thirty, isn't there?' 'I should think *so*,' she says, with a falling emphasis on the 'so', which makes her reply sound gentler and more reassuring than the breezier, English, 'I should *think* so.' There was also something pleasant, at least to me, in the suggestion of social and spiritual cohesion in the assumption made by both of them, pretty girl and simpleton, that each would formally celebrate, in the same fashion, the nature of that particular day. Both of them seemed to know who they were, and where they stood in relation to something outside themselves. That is not common.

'We want more village idiots over here,' said the joker Oliver St John Gogarty, exasperated with life in 1920s London. 'I cannot bear unmitigated facts for long. What is wrong here, I thought, is the absence of metaphysical man. We want more village idiots over here. A country without village idiots is not worth living in.' One way of expressing Irish impatience with, in the end, too much English good sense.

That the immigrant Irish have infected the Australian character not only with a dislike of authority but also with what could be called 'the pleasures of fancifulness' is to be doubted. In both antipodean countries you are expected to say what you mean; hints, signalled evasiveness, ironies, are greeted with the Australian Pause. After Europe such directness can feel restful, but it is also dangerous. When nothing is allowed to be merely suggested, you can, in such plain speaking, begin with a tiny misunderstanding, of colour and tone, and this can increase, as lines can diverge, until misunderstanding, the gap between you and your companion, is too great to resolve. You thought you understood each other, but you didn't at all.

I had arranged somewhere to stay on my second night in Auckland; on the first evening I had hoped to be free to wander on my own, sniffing the place. However, it was late when I arrived and the taxi-driver from the airport, who was very drunk, a large man whom I took to be a Maori, wanted to know *exactly* what kind of hotel I wanted to be taken to. By now I knew that anything other than brutal directness would cause confusion, so I said: 'Quiet and cheap.' '*How* quiet?' he said, trying in vain to focus on my face in his driving-mirror. '*Very* quiet,' I answered, with regret, but fine shades were useless here. Perhaps I overdid the directness because he drove me to a hotel run by the Salvation Army. There were signs on the bedroom wall forbidding the importation of alcohol, and other admonitions. It was not a promising beginning, in a town my father had left behind as a young man, and about which he had never felt impelled to say much.

Apart from his affection for the Maoris – as a child I remember playing with beautiful objects of greenstone, inherited from his father, but lost with the rest of our possessions in a 1940 air raid – my father never spoke of his New Zealand life, or I do not remember his doing so; but he always tried to help Australians and New Zealanders in his line of show-business when they came to work in England.

Without stories from him, I had acquired a picture of a quiet, uneventful place, covered in sheep, supplanted in his affection by clubbable, pubbable London. But in Australasia the hotels leave a copy of the local paper outside your door, and it was a disappointment to see the headline on my first morning, 'Rape, Sexual Abuse, Reaching Crisis Stage'. I might as well have been at home. The figures were bad, but it was also the tone that was reminiscent of England, a flurry of gloom and statistics which could only dismay and which also somehow managed to make the reader wonder if he was not being shocked on purpose to sell the paper: 'One in every four girls and one in every nine boys is likely to be molested before the age of 16.' So *many*? And what did 'molested', in this case, mean? Clearly, if this was anything to go by, New Zealand was going to be no different in its alarms and preoccupations, and silliness, from just about everywhere else in the world. I realised that I had half hoped for a place of freshness and innocence retained, of bronzed young people from the New World who might be able to cleanse and revitalise the Old.

I read on, among the rape statistics: 17 per cent were committed by Maoris, 66 per cent by Pakeha, 'and the rest by Pacific Island or other nationalities'. There was comfort to be gained from the word 'Pakeha', the Maori name for the white man, for it seemed to put the two races verbally on an equal footing. What I could not know on that first morning was the significance of the 'Pacific Islands' reference. 'The Islanders' – from Samoa, Tonga and smaller islands – had arrived of late in great numbers, and there was so little employment for them that there was trouble not only between them and the Pakeha but between them and the Maoris. The very word 'Islander' could cause a grimness to settle on the mouth of a white, middle-class Aucklander. They were thought to be wrecking the place.

Patrick and his family had stayed with Father James Paul at his parish of Onehunga, then a few miles from Auckland, but now not outside it at all because Auckland, a city of about 300,000 inhabitants, has spilt itself gigantically into an area the size of Greater London. Onehunga, on the sea, once reasonably prosperous, is now a mess, a sprawl of decaying bungalows, seedy takeaways, broken-down repair shops. 'Islanders!' was the only comment of my Pakeha companion looking at the decay.

Father Paul – arriving from Carlow in 1856, he was not the first priest, but could be thought of as a pioneer – was obviously a man of energy. Over the years he succeeded in having his own large church built, and in paying for it; large enough for Bishop Pompallier to consider nominating it as his cathedral, until it was decided it was too far from the centre of Auckland. 'Five thousand people attended his funeral,' I was told, and was shown a photograph of him, the man who had helped, perhaps rescued, Patrick after his long sojourn in Van Diemen's Land. In his biretta, hair crisply curling on either side of it, he had the strength, humour and handsomeness of Spencer Tracy in one of his priestly roles; I was inclined to make a hero of Father Paul, and when I later read his diaries I decided he was one.

He was buried under the altar of the church he had spent his life building, but now, because of Vatican II, the altar has been moved to a central position and he is under carpet-squares.

The elderly native-born priest who showed us round, whom we had unintentionally roused from his siesta in the large, decrepit presbytery nearby, had barely heard of him. This was perhaps not surprising, since my interest was specialised, but it was sad. Priests are seldom concerned with the human past; their concern is, I hope, with the slow unfolding of God's will. It was only I, a brief visitor from a distant, secular world, who cared about the carpet-squares; doubtless Father Paul did not mind. Priests are also concerned with the practical present. This one's largely 'Islander' congregation was trying to force him (a Pakeha) to say the Mass in Samoan. 'No, no,' he had said. 'You can have your vernacular hymns if you like.' Vatican II and ethnic self-consciousness were making life as difficult for priests in New Zealand as it was everywhere else.

The holes in his cardigan, the holes in the walls of his originally elegant presbytery, whether these indicated holy poverty or the running-down of Catholicism in New Zealand, it was difficult to judge. Possibly both; New Zealand priests had voted themselves annual salaries the equivalent of £750 a year – New Zealand is an expensive place – in order to keep them on a level with their poorer parishioners; this was noble of them, nevertheless there grew an impression that the early missionary activities of such as Father Paul have not fallen, in New Zealand, on particularly fertile ground. It is a utilitarian country; in that way is like the rest of the modern Western world.

Outside the church were the red headstones of Patrick and Margaret, his carved death-date wrong by two years, 1905 when it should be 1907: 'Never trust a headstone,' I was told, and I wondered again what there was to trust, in an investigation of the past. The last place I had been in that I knew for sure was associated with these two (their names in the marriage register, and perhaps one could trust that) was the cathedral at Carlow, where they were so young, so many years before, so far away. There I had tried to pray and think about those two unimaginable young strangers with whom I knew I was connected. Here, at the end of their story, there seemed nothing better to do than take a photograph of their headstones. As the search, such as it was, approached the present, there was beginning to be something disturbing about it, as though I might be coming near old confusions, best left to their sleep.

One day we went (I had now made contact with a kinswoman, Diane Wilson, also descended from Patrick and Margaret, Mary Ann her great-grandmother) to seek out the graves of my grandfather and grandmother. That day, in that windswept place, we failed to find them, and in an obscure way I was relieved. It seemed that I was now tinkering too much with lives, and deaths, closer in time but still so difficult imaginatively to enter that I could offer them nothing but an abstract, stranger's respect. They were best left to themselves, and to those who had known them.

Through Diane I was now meeting all sorts of people – though there were no longer any Kavanaghs – with whom I shared Patrick as a great-grandfather. I could make little of this, they were all so different from each other. I cannot imagine that I had expected otherwise, but I have never been part of any extended family or system of kinship, and had sometimes a little envied those who appeared to have these things. Apart from anything else such a system of kin removed some of the burden of choice. You could still choose your friends, but there was also this large, various group which was simply there, given, which must save trouble. But now, looking round a room crowded with these kin, I could sense no connection, between them or with me; time and space had intervened too firmly. Just as Patrick had let down the historian Geoffrey Stillwell by leaving Tasmania, otherwise he would have been able to tell all about him, so had my father as it were let down these people by leaving New Zealand, and I was the inheritor of that disconnection.

The one thing nearly all of them had in common was a degree of prosperity. At first I wondered about this, then I thought I understood. Some of them, doubtless, were prosperous through their own efforts, but there was an effortless, though democratic, sense of wealth about the others that was, I suddenly saw, based on *land*. They, or rather Patrick, and the people his children had married, had got here first.

Land is the gold standard of New Zealand. 'Sections' (of land), as they are called, have gone up and up in value recently, especially if they are in or near towns. Sections acquired long ago, now sold or subdivided, were gold mines. This was unsettling, not because I blamed these folk, these kin, but it seemed a rickety foundation for a whole economy. New Zealand, far from being the secure haven I had half expected to find, was unusually fragile.

As I travelled around I also came to feel there was something missing in the place – missing also in contemporary England, but England is older and more various – something even more fundamental than the faith Father Paul had tried to help implant a hundred years before, something Oliver St John Gogarty may have meant by 'the absence of metaphysical man'. The presence of that sort of spirituality, speculativeness, is perhaps dependent on a long and complex history – which makes 'direct' speaking impossible, as well as no fun – and on widespread freedom among the people from the distractions of wealth: as in Ireland. ('Travel light' had been my father's constant exhortation.) I sensed this absence, of another dimension, as I have done in England, therefore I began to wonder to myself – (why not, in such circumstances, be fanciful) – whether, in respect of genes, I had ever left Carlow at all.

I had come to New Zealand without Old World snobbery – the opposite, or that snobbery inverted; I wanted to find in it a source of rejuvenation for jaded Europe, and for Polynesia, if that was required; a South Sea island with European traditions and skills refreshed, transformed. It is not like that. There were positives to remark on, but the disappointment came first.

People had not come to New Zealand for religious or political reasons, at least not to the North Island; they were fleeing no persecution. They had come to better themselves.

Perhaps in this respect the Irish immigrants had an advantage. They could at least feel, or pretend, they had been driven from the land of their birth, had had no choice. But for those who had come to improve their lot, and had succeeded in doing so, the question faced their descendants in a secular age: what now? It takes a long time for a tradition of *noblesse oblige* to establish itself, time for respect for things of the mind to grow, or lip-service to them; even for conspicuous consumption to be understood. Such things became the badges and duties of the fortunate in Renaissance Europe and in every part of the long-settled world, including Polynesia. Even in the most primitive societies chiefs have bigger houses, bigger stomachs, bigger wives, and there are ceremonies and rituals that go along with these things. But the genuine democracy of urban New Zealand works against this kind of response and responsibility among the wealthy, because they must be no different from anyone else – not a bit of it, mate – they just have more.

This is not a problem confined to New Zealand, and perhaps in New Zealand it is particularly early days. A native historian reminded me impatiently that it had taken England a thousand years to absorb all her influences. In that sense New Zealand had already done well: 'When we go to England or Ireland', he said, 'we know we are a different people.' But precisely because New Zealand is new, a fresh start, the irritating question asserts itself nakedly, and not overlaid by history: After a point, what do we better ourselves *for*? I could hear no answer. This was the place where the bones of my recent ancestors lay. What had grown out of the soil their work and their bodies had enriched, apart from this silence, possibly this blank? The question made me haunt bookshops and churches in an attempt to find out what people here believed. You could not ask them directly, less so here than anywhere. One friend told me, unasked, that he intended to spend the evening memorising the secret measurements of King Solomon's temple.

The layout of Auckland itself might have been purposely designed to prevent any possibility of such social or spiritual answering: as in the States, it forces almost everyone into his own separations. From the extinct green volcano, Mount Eden, carved with Maori earthworks, the town stretches way beyond the horizon on every side, a small town which is almost the size of an English county, an endless series of suburbs that radiate from no centre. There is little public transport and taxis thrive, mostly driven by Samoans or Tongans whose English is not good. There is a downtown Auckland, by the sea, but that is mostly being pulled down. 'Eighteen cranes at work in the town today!' said a rare Pakeha taxi-driver, who clearly approved. What is old is being replaced by the international-anonymous, and here the developers hold a trump: whatever some might wish to preserve can be designated 'an earthquake hazard'. This taxi-driver was wearing shorts and sat comfortably askew, one bare knee propped against the dashboard. 'Soon be finished for today. Then it's down to the pool and the barbecue!' He, at least, knew what he liked about New Zealand, and no one would grudge it him. Someone else said they liked the place because they could swim in warm sea in the morning and ski in the afternoon. 'But', she added, 'we are an ugly race. Grey.'

That is not true. Yet even handsome Australasians, especially young women, pull faces, grimace, which gives the impression of a lack of self-assurance, an absence of repose. In this connection, and to a remarkable degree, they wonder aloud who they are. One South African-Dutch-Welsh-New Zealander put it bluntly: 'Who is what?'

Perhaps the early New Zealand of Father Paul, and Patrick, was calmer, still warm with old roots. Father Ernest Simmons, the diocesan archivist, to whom I had written before I left England, said that James Paul would have had a glebe of maybe five acres, with cottages on it, and he could easily have put up Patrick and his family. Such family migrations, kinship hospitalities deriving from the Old World, were commonplace in new countries; there was nothing of the status of refugee about their arrival. 1866 was a good time to come, the end of the Maori Wars period, gold was being found, timber was needed for the mines, shops for the miners. Father Simmons reckoned that Father Paul had tipped off his brother-in-law that New Zealand was the place to be.

In 1868 there is a record that Patrick bought a small patch of land at Patumahoe, and with his grown sons (my grandfather would have been around twenty-five) he must have farmed that and anywhere else he could get hold of. I wanted to find out how he had finished up, how the journey from Carlow had ended.

Diane Wilson knew. She drove me to Helensville, to the house, 'Te Makiri', she had loved as a girl, where Patrick had spent a proportion of his last years after Margaret died in 1872. About thirty miles from Auckland, deep in Irish-looking countryside, it is a beautiful old place.

Mary Ann, the infant who came out on the *Arab*, four years after arriving in New Zealand married an Irishman, James Hand, who had, or acquired later, about 4000 acres of land around Helensville and the elegant, white-painted Tolstoyan house, built on a small bluff above the river; the name means 'stream'. The view from its veranda, surprisingly in that volcanic island, is once again reminiscent of Carlow. The old man may have been miserable for all I can tell, but it is a good place, and good to think of him sitting there.

He outlived his daughter Mary Ann. She died in 1891 and is buried in a little fenced family plot on the hillside. My father would have known the house; he was fifteen when Patrick died. Here at last was a link, my young father making a bridge, as it were, from Carlow to me.

After Mary Ann died, Patrick stayed on there with his widowed son-in-law, at least for periods. They were looked after by a housekeeper, Miss Morgan, who came from the orphanage founded by Father Paul. So do they join together, the Irish kinships, and there are those who were alive until recently who remembered Mary Ann's children musing in old age about Borris, in Carlow, which they never saw. In those days tradition, become oral as among Maoris, must have helped to hold things together.

That is a point at which to leave Patrick, now become patriarch, except for a note about him that appeared in the obituary of his son, my grandfather, in 1926.

Mr Patrick Kavanagh, father of the deceased, settled at

Patumahoe in 1866. In his early days Mr Kavanagh carried on his trade of carpenter and builder, and among his works was the original Patumahoe Hall. He also specialised in the construction of water wheels, and those of most of the flax mills which were formerly dotted about in Mauku and Waiuku were the work of his hands.

So the 'groom', the 'baker', the man of any occupation or none, had all the time been a carpenter? I hope it is true, because it is hard to think of many things more useful or pleasant, or more fun to make, than water-wheels.

The Hands, and Mary Ann, seemed to have owned just about the whole of the little township of Helensville: the sawmill (my grandfather ran that), the butcher's (one of his brothers), the hotel (owned, and possibly run, by Mary Ann). 'They just rolled up their sleeves,' said Diane. That is what must have been good about early New Zealand. It may have been greedy to keep everything in the family, but at least they did the work themselves and there was no ambition to play the squire.

It was my grandfather's job, later, to oversee the distribution of land and save it from falling into the hands of land-agglomerators, and thus prevent the creation of a landowning class. The government instigator of that scheme, John McKenzie, was the son of an evicted Highland crofter. The Old World did not only throw an inhibiting shadow over the New. It had taught hard lessons, and these had been learned.

15

Ponsonby

It was good to think of the Carlow man making water-wheels in country places with Maori names, but they were places from which the Maoris had been more or less excluded. As we stood on the smooth, sculpted green of Mount Eden, once a Maori *pa* or fortified place – Captain Cook had marvelled at the ingenuity of Maori forts – looking down over spreading Auckland, listening to the cries of Japanese tourists as they climbed from their motor coaches, a Pakeha friend told me that he liked the Maoris, they were generous, goodnatured people, but this somehow always left them at the bottom of the heap.

While I was there they were demanding control over their old fishing-grounds, far out to sea, and the Pakeha objection was that they had fished by canoe, not the miles offshore made possible by powerful engines. Maybe, but the earliest explorers could hardly credit Maori dexterity with their canoes. They had found New Zealand, uninhabited, eight or nine hundred years before the first white man, and had travelled thousands of miles in their canoes to do so.

'Never accept an organ transplant from a Maori – he'll want it back!' The cheerful white taxi-driver in shorts had told me that one, in Auckland. In Helensville, in Mary Ann's hotel, thirty miles away, I was told it again the same day; it was the latest. Each time the white tellers were careful to say that Maori friends had enjoyed the joke as much as they had. That week a Maori activist, Hana Te Hanara, in a speech at Auckland University, was alleged to have said, 'Kill a white man and make yourself a hero.' It was not how my father had described the relationship with the Maoris; he had said they were friends. In fact, even now, Hana Te Hanara was laughed away by white New Zealanders, because her Maori father had been chief of staff of the New Zealand army – some said she was only half Maori anyway, the other half being Irish.

While I was learning about these things I stayed in one of the leafy suburbs, where you do not see Maoris, or Islanders. A previous occupant of my room had told my hosts, making them nervous, that he had been at school with me and that there I had been a 'wild Irishman'. The stereotypes cling, but the quietness of where I was living was tempting me to become one.

By great good fortune, through a friend in England, I was lent a house in 'the Ponsonby area' and the taxi-driver who took me there did so doubtfully. I asked her why, and she replied candidly: 'Too full of the kind of people I dislike.' Perhaps she meant the dark faces, perhaps not; it had a raffish air. She told me I was unlikely to find anywhere to eat on a Sunday – 'You're lucky if a parachute opens on a Sunday,' somebody else had said – but on Ponsonby Road there were open restaurants, late-night Asian delicatessens, esoteric bookshops; a kind of Auckland Putney, in fact.

The luck continued. It turned out to be where my grand-parents and father had lived before the First World War; it had now come down in the world. My father had gone to school at the Sacred Heart College, at that time just round the corner from the house I had been lent. Their family house was in St Mary's Road, overlooking the bay, a little way along the street. Near their house was the Bishop's Palace – now democratised, called the Bishop's House – and I knew my grandfather had chosen and donated the timber for that, because I had read so in one of his obituaries. I looked forward to calling on the archivist there, Father Simmons, for surely there, if anywhere,

anywhere, I might find a representative of New Zealand 'metaphysical man'.

Before I did so, on the day appointed, I went in search of a bottle of whisky, for the metaphysical evening.

On Ponsonby Road, at an intersection, bedecked with bunting and with every kind of cut-price enticement advertised in its windows was 'The 8 Litre Discount Bottle Shop'. I went in and was told I could only buy eight litres of it, or of any alcoholic drink, which could include whisky. It was not my first experience of the baffling, foreign, *inconvenience* of New Zealand. It takes time to find your way about any unknown country (in Milan you have to buy your tram ticket in advance, at a tobacconist) but the snags in New Zealand were unlike those in any other place. There are no telephones in the pubs, for example; indeed, there are no pubs, or very few.

There was nothing for it, if I wanted the whisky, but to seek help, find a familiar face in a street where I knew no one. So I approached the first, aged, Irish-looking man I saw and asked him where I could buy a bottle of whisky and not eight litres of it. He laid a hand on my arm and answered, 'Now, you just go down the street, past those two pillars there – you see them? – and there you'll find a place that will sell you as much, or as little, whisky as you want.' The carefulness of the instruction, and the cadence, were both as Irish as his accent.

How had I recognised him?

Dervla Murphy has written that whenever she is in London she makes an experiment: she goes up to an Irish-looking person and asks the way; in 95 per cent of cases, she says, she is right, the person answers in an Irish accent. She cannot understand this, because she does not believe there is a distinctive Irish face. She concludes, helplessly, 'it must be something in the eyes', as though 'Irishness', now spread so widely about the world, 'has somehow retreated within'. (As for the spreading of the Irish, the historian R. F. Foster comes up with an astonishing statistic: by 1890, thirty-nine out of every hundred people who had been born in Ireland were living outside it.) Whether there is an Irish face, I do not know. Some believe so. Long ago, in a late-night café in Ostia Antica, near Rome, I was approached by a man who asked me in careful English if I was Irish. Not an easy question to answer, in my case, so I asked him why he wanted to know. He said he was a Jew, on his way to Canada, allowed out of Russia for the first time, and I corresponded to the idea he had formed in Russia of an Irishman. So I told him he was right.

Certainly, in terms of the women my sires had married – the Pauls, the Lorigans, the O'Keefes – I am Irish by blood, whatever that means. When I told my father I wanted to marry Sally – Welsh-Scottish-American-German-Jewish-Protestant – expecting him to be concerned about the last condition, he said: 'Time there was some fresh blood in the family.'

'Ever met a pure-bred Maori?' said Father Simmons at once, in the Bishop's House, introducing me to the housekeeper, who was laughing. 'Can you tell the difference?'

'I *think* so,' I said, and I had in fact been trying to distinguish between Maoris and Islanders in the street.

'Well you can't; no one can. Mary's a Samoan.'

A man to be watched, Father Simmons. With that small trick he had already disposed of the possibly poisonous distinction being drawn in the public mind between Islanders – thought to be the source of drugs, gangs, violence – and the decent (of course, Pakeha-influenced) Maoris.

I followed him up the stairs, paying attention to the banisters, made of wood chosen and donated by my grandfather. In the large reception room (with its heavy doors of Kauri-wood), cheerless as all such presbytery rooms are – priests lead hard lives – it was Father Simmons who told me of the glebe at Onehunga with its cottages, and of how Father Paul could have housed the Kavanaghs. It was also Simmons who said that no Irishman takes seriously what he puts on a piece of government paper – which reduced, if it did not clear up, the Church of Ireland/Roman Catholic confusion of the Tasmanian census returns.

When I deplored the way Father Paul's grave was unmarked and was now under carpet-squares, he showed signs of impatience. 'He was an ordinary hard-working Irish priest. I'm of English stock. I've researched my ancestors in Cornwall.' I was not going to be allowed any racial conspiracy here. The impatience was perhaps an echo of an old disgruntlement, at the way the Irish had seemed to hijack Catholicism in the early days, perhaps even Christianity itself – 'the faith of Ireland and the Gospel of Erin'.

It was on visits to England that New Zealanders like him knew they had become 'a different people'; it was Father Simmons who said that. I asked him about the Sacred Heart on Ponsonby Street, where my grandfather had had his Requiem Mass; it must have been the Kavanagh parish church, and I had not been able to find it. 'Forget about the Sacred Heart,' he said, impatient again. 'I was curate there. It's gone.' I asked him where it had been and it became clear from his description that it had been on the site of 'The 8 Litre Discount Bottle Shop'.

My father would have enjoyed that, in his way. I could hear his shade coaxing me to come away from all this, 'Leave it, leave it.' But it was too late, I was embarked. I left Father Simmons a book of my poems, as some sort of guarantee of seriousness, my bona fides, and he promised to look out Father Paul's diaries and some old books of the period.

After I left him (the way was past the comfortable house my father lived in as a boy) I wondered whether I should write a book called 'The 8 Litre Discount Bottle Shop', *à la* Tom Wolfe, about the futility of all searches of the past, such as mine, when things are swept away so fast. I wandered along my father's road, then along Ponsonby Street, remarking anything that he might have seen as a boy on his way to school. Or was he a boarder? It seemed unlikely, when his home was so near; but I remembered his telling me – so he did after all sometimes speak of his life in New Zealand – about a country boy he and his fellow boarders told to blow out the dormitory electric light, and the boy had tried. St Mary's Road must have been pleasant then, with a view of St Mary's Bay, and the steam ships and sailing ships and scows. Some of the boys came to school by ship. Now, with land reclamation, and marinas and the long Auckland Bridge, the sea is difficult to glimpse. The Sacred Heart College is no longer in Richmond Road, and its playing fields are built over. It has removed itself to a green site at the far edge of town. There I was shown the school magazine which my father had coedited. It seemed extra-ordinarily literate. Could the boys nowadays write like that? 'They are good at other things. Computers?' The Marist Brother Maurice invited me to lunch, but the cooking smells in the refectory reminded me too much of my own boarding-school.

Because of New Zealand interest in my father I was interviewed by the *New Zealand Herald* and as a consequence, later, after I had left, I received letters from people who had known him, or of him, or known his brother Paul who died in Wellington in 1962. One letter took exception to a phrase in the article which appeared to suggest that my father had only become funny when he wrote the wartime radio show, *Itma*, in England. On the contrary, he had been funny in New Zealand, at school, 'his patter was repeated for years, always to laughter', but unfortunately, as is the way of things, the writer could not remember what the patter was. I even heard from one of my father's godsons, whom a better investigator than I might have known about and tracked down. He wrote, a little grimly but no doubt accurately:

The old Sacred Heart College in Richmond Road was a fairly rugged institution, staffed by rugged Marist Brothers, and with an even more rugged roll of pupils. Rugby, discipline, hard work, the cane. I would hazard a guess that your father found both his primary school years and secondary school years painful rather than pleasant. . . . Old Ponsonby was full of the Irish. Just look at the street names, Dublin Street, St Francis de Sales Street, Emmet Street, Sarsfield Street. At one time (the 1920s and earlier) Sacred Heart parish [the 8 Litre Discount Bottle Shop] was the biggest Catholic parish in New Zealand. Most of our priests were from Ireland. . . . Your father *must* have been conscious of the Irish political opposition to the English parliament, the ambivalent stance of Irish-descended NZ Catholics who (later) volunteered, or were conscripted in WWI; and of some of the West Coast Irish who chose to 'go bush' rather than fight for the English oppressor, in WWI. I remark on this because your father's views seem to have been those of a man conservative (English conservative) in politics, but with the Irishman's sharp eye for eccentricities of English behaviour.

That seems about right. The godson, Bob Cotterall, goes on gently to lament 'the thundering march of progress that has swept old Ponsonby away', even the disappearance of the lamp from outside the Ponsonby Club Hotel (which became my pub, or the nearest to a pub I could find).

Yes, 'the thundering march of progress', but back in the borrowed house I listened in near disbelief to a repeat of *Send for Paul Temple* on the radio, a programme I had last heard as a boy, when people spoke as no one does in England anymore, clipped, as though afraid to let too wide a gap appear between their teeth; there were also endless requests for Gracie Fields. But that was the radio. On television there was a New Zealand version of a satirical programme popular in England, *Spitting Image*, which lampooned their local politicians, and it was more tightly aimed, bit deeper, than the grapeshot coarseness of its English counterpart.

I had dinner with Mervyn Poland, Diane Wilson's father, at his 'gracious residence' (it was the Pakeha taxi-driver who called it that, respectfully). We had Patrick Kavanagh as a great-grandfather in common, for Mervyn is grandson of Mary Ann, of the *Arab*. Blue Irish eyes, a recognisable 'Old World' type; Irish teasing, Irish interest in horses; we watched videos of his racehorse, Seeyoulater, almost, but never quite, winning. (Great-grandson of a groom? – or of a baker, or maker of water-wheels? 'They just rolled up their sleeves,' Diane had said.)

But apart from Diane and her father, the rest of the kinsfolk were not, to me, recognisable as 'Old World' types, nor would they want to be. They had become 'a different people'. The sense of Irishness seems to have evaporated, the Catholicism too, perhaps, in some of them, and the cohesiveness these things must have given. Probably it was inevitable and possibly it is good, the past and the present refusing to show a series of evident connections.

In the library of the Bishop's House I read, in a book called *Old Waikito Days*, of 'Mr Kavanagh's hospitable residence at Patumahoe. The original Mr Kavanagh was hale and hearty at that time. [1880; he must have been in his early sixties]. Mrs Kavanagh had died some years previously. Miss Kavanagh and Henry and Terence Kavanagh, of Ponsonby, are survivors of that fine old stock.' Henry was my grandfather. Scant materials out of which to make bricks.

But Father Paul's diary fascinated, because of what it revealed about the practicality, in promulgation of a mystery, of a priest's life. He notes the progress of the building of the church, the cost, other parish accounts, and then 'brought SS to Mrs Southern', his invariable way of referring to the sacrament, the *sanctissimum sacramentum*, taking communion to those unable to get to church, who mostly sound poor. A daily mixture of the practical and the spiritual expressed in ritual: the sort of thing you find in Homer, which is why there is such a strong sense of a complete world in Homer. 'Aug 20. 1889. Mass. To Helensville by the 9.50 train. Find James Hand all but dead – sat up with him all night.' That was Mary Ann's husband, in Te Makiri, the pretty white house – Mervyn's grandfather; at the funeral, says Father Paul, was 'Harry', who was mine.

Sitting in the library talking, fiddling with a rarely lit pipe, Father Simmons revealed the millennial, even eternal, perspective that most priests use, so that contemporary babble falls away. If things do not seem good for Christianity now, that will be only temporary, or perhaps they are good, in wider terms than we can understand. After two thousand years God will not let anything seriously disturb his purpose. Father Simmons was interested in the effect Maori spirituality was having on New Zealand Christianity. 'In two hundred years New Zealand will be English-Polynesian. How long did it take England to absorb influences and develop? Longer than that!'

I asked him about my grandfather's generosity to the church. He gave it everything he had. Was it perhaps to earn himself respectability?

'Among ten per cent of the population? Look, you have to be resigned to the fact that most people don't give a damn about Christianity. It was reactionary liberals who came to New Zealand. The faith was kept alive by people like your grandfather.'

'Giving it all away when his son and grandchild were starving in London?' It was a question designed to rattle him. I felt it was my turn to do some bringing back to earth.

He stared, and gave the only possible reply: 'That is for you to decide. To say Mass is the most important thing in my life. And to preach the Gospel, in whatever way, in my books.'

He went off to buy whisky for some bishops who were staying

staying in the House for a conference; his life a mixture of the
mysterious – the Mass, the Gospel – and the practical.

While he was gone I became more aware that the chairs in
the library were covered with various kinds of bishops' regalia,
copes and mitres and so on, presumably for some sort of
ceremony next day. I was not sure, but I thought I could see a
cardinal's hat. The sun, coming in through the high windows
in rays, mote-laden, made them look threadbare and tawdry,
absurd, the props for a play by Jean Genet. Next day these men
would be parading *en travestie*. What did it all matter? It was a
charade, a joke in bad taste, a bogus imposition of Authority.
This was a perception that is easier to come upon in New
Zealand than elsewhere, because there is so little accretion of
time on the surface there; the bare bones show through, and
mock.

Not that New Zealand is to blame. That country was
becoming for me, as I had suspected it would, a metaphor for
contemporary secular rootlessness, just as my search for my
family was a metaphor, a hunt for a lost connection, 'Dimly
divined but keenly / Felt with a phantom hunger'; and no more
than Louis MacNeice did I think I would find it, or at least not
in a form I would at once recognise. But the search itself was a
form of connection, in the feeling required to make it, and in
what happened on the way. The searcher must also be
prepared to face the discovery that there are no connections at
all, only mummery.

'To say Mass is the most important thing in my life. And to
preach the Gospel.' It had been impossible to doubt the
sincerity of that: a priest nearing the end of his career, and
unshaken.

He had left me with a photocopy of one of my grandfather's
obituaries. 'Mr Kavanagh was a collector of Maori curios, and
anything connected with the early history of New Zealand. He
was also keenly interested in Roman Catholic educational
institutions, and established a very valuable museum at the

College of the Sacred Heart. He presented collections of ethnological value to many convents in the city and suburbs.' Father Simmons had thought the main collection had been sold by the Marist brothers to endow scholarships, and the rest was on loan to the Auckland Museum.

This is an enormous, handsome building set on a green knoll in the middle of 'the Domain', the central park. It is also a magnificent museum, imaginatively laid out and lit. The guides are young Maori women in some long ethnic costume, scarlet and white, with scarlet headbands. One was saying to a group round a model of a Maori fort, 'You have to remember, we were a very warlike people.'

I had been warned in England about the impact the Maori canoes make, the first time you see them, but I was still unprepared. They bring tears to the eyes and it is difficult to say why. They are small, sometimes with outriggers lashed to them, and give an impression of fragility and balance, of man's ingeniousness and courage, and on their unpainted light-brown wood there is a patina of use, of bare hands and feet. Their simplicity and appropriateness touch some forgotten nerve.

My grandfather's collection, now the Marist Collection, was mostly in store, since there is so much of it. If this is merely the remains of one collection, he must have collected obsessively – hundreds of spears, clubs, ceremonial staffs, superb greenstone axeheads, little carved *tikis*. What pieces there were on display, about a tenth of it, were often the star items, in the centre of their case. My grandfather was not as I had imagined him.

More and more I saw that New Zealand was not as I had imagined it, either. One evening I sat in the erstwhile Ponsonby Club Hotel, now a bar, reading a book by Father Simmons called *God Became Man*, and drinking Australian chablis. If you asked yourself the question, as I had, 'What do we better ourselves for?' or (better) 'What are *we* for?', Father Simmons set out to answer, metaphysically. It was exactly the sort of book that was needed, non-sectarian, including within a traditionally Christian, spiritually directed view of life the discoveries of science and psychology, and always aware that some had not 'bettered themselves' at all, and never would. The spiritualities of the Maoris and Islanders were as prominently on stage as those of the Pakeha. Given the acceptance (wide and generous) of the basic premise, they blended together and enriched each other. It was an expression of the priest's intelligence, experience and faith.

A shadow fell across the book, and an arm. 'I'm Tongan. You like Tongans? My name Denis. Where your girlfriend? I get you girlfriend.' He was very big and very drunk.

Uneasily aware of his size I said, 'Denis, you're drunk. I'm reading.'

He swayed a little, his arm still resting across the book, but more, I thought, to stop him falling over than from aggression. 'You wait here. I get my sister.'

He went off and I continued to read, defiantly. He had seemed genial enough, which is why I had risked saying what I did, hoping it would work and he would go away. But doubts began to form themselves between me and Father Simmons's pages. Suppose he did come back, with his sister, or whoever? If I turned her down there might be a fracas. Would anybody in that reasonably respectable pub help me out of that? No one seemed to have noticed him lurching all over me. Perhaps they were interested to see how the Pom dug himself out of this one. Damn. Blue eyes, brown eyes, it doesn't matter, a pest is a pest; I had to leave, in case he did come back; he had driven me out.

The sins of the great-grandfathers are visited on the sons. I doubt that Maoris disturbed my great-grandfather, on Maori land, as he built his water-wheels. White man's culture displaces other cultures, then a time comes when these try to join his, which has no place for them, not in New Zealand, no jobs anyway, and they are forced to what desperate shifts they can find, and there will be no end to this.

Next day was Sunday and I went to the small, over-modern, concrete wigwam of a church near the borrowed house – the Sacred Heart, replacing the one my father would have known, but on a different site. I had often passed a handpainted sign, 'Sister Disciples of the Divine Lord', on the gatepost of a house opposite, which sounded queer; Ponsonby was a great place for odd sects. But no, they were nuns, Roman Catholic and black; they had joined the white man's culture, or the foundations of it, which is supposed to belong to everyone.

The words of the hymns and the liturgical responses were cast on the whitewashed wall behind the altar by a magic lantern, nun-operated, and we were gently rehearsed in them before Mass began. Most of the congregation were black, but not all. They looked beautiful and devout, those black nuns in their white wimples, and I began to feel tears in my eyes again, as I had at the sight of the Maori canoes. I was becoming worse than Berlioz. Like the canoes, the nuns had an appropriate simplicity, a seriousness that seems often lost in the old world. Perhaps other peoples will help us to regain these things.

16

Henry Paul

It had somehow filtered through to my young self, without anything disloyal being said, that my grandfather, Henry Paul Kavanagh, had been a difficult man, to say the least. Probably this was because of my mother's tales of early hardship, before I was born, when money ceased to come from New Zealand. As I approached nearer that time, in imagination and investigation, I began to hesitate. I suspected I might be coming near old family unhappinesses, injustices, even scandals. It was not as though my father's ghost, under the flagstones, was whispering hoarsely, 'Revenge!' On the contrary, I had almost heard him begging me to stop.

However, I was now long embarked, and had learned that my grandfather had worked for the government in the last years of his career and therefore had a government file in Wellington. The prospect of holding in my hand some hard facts, and of being able to rest for a moment from mere speculation, was irresistible, so I flew down to Wellington, on the far tip of the North Island.

Old journalistic hands had told me to get as much local publicity for my quest as I could, because then people write in with information, which certainly turned out to be the case after the interview with the *New Zealand Herald*. Not I, but my father, was the point of interest, and this made it easier to push myself in this way; so I arranged to be interviewed about him by *The New Zealand Listener* in Wellington. The young journalist I talked to in the Wellington hotel knew that at this time I wrote a weekly column for the London *Spectator* and he asked what its circulation was. I answered proudly that I thought it had risen to 35,000 copies (it had recently doubled from 17,000), and he was incredulous, because his magazine had a circulation of two million. Admittedly, it also gave the times of all radio and television programmes, and would often be bought for that reason alone, but it is a serious and entertaining magazine with a hefty books and arts coverage. To think of it in the hands of most of the population every week was encouraging, given the situation in Britain, where a handful of people read the (variably) 'serious' papers and the rest nothing, or *The Sun*. The young journalist (it is important that he was young) took me on a short tour of his town and told me of places it would be unwise to walk in late at night. In *Wellington*? Or does danger and crime give towns some sort of big-city status? He was in a condition of exasperation about what was happening to his city. We counted seven huge tower-cranes in the centre of it, resting for the evening; not so many as in Auckland, but enough. 'It certainly pisses *me* off!' he said. 'They're replacing that' – he pointed to a distinctive building in Victorian Gothic – 'with that!' – the usual blank stare of glass and concrete. 'They're taking away my *identity*!' He shrugged impatiently, supposed it was something to do with being a new country. But a new country the uprooted fathers built; and for their descendants to see their building uprooted must be particularly hard.

It is hard in old countries too, but perhaps our sense of identity is harder-set, and more that is old is passed over. In New Zealand the pace of city change hits you more quickly, as do other things which could happen anywhere but seem highlighted by their happening in New Zealand.

For example, next morning, not thirty seconds out of the hotel, on the way to the library, a man approached me directly, very fast, on a narrow path between the flower-beds. He had olive skin and eyes of such startling jet, with a look so cold in them, directed towards me, that it chilled. There was no question but he intended to walk straight through me if I did not step aside on to the grass, so I did, and he strode on, not breaking his pace, not looking back. He had seemed not murderous exactly, but outside the frame, a man who had looked after himself in a hostile world from the day he could walk.

In the library, by contrast, all was scholarly and gentle, but the file I sought was not there; it was on the other side of town. On my way, in Cuba Street (one of the places I had been warned not to wander in at night), I saw the apparition again, hung with a guitar, surrounded by women in long, brightly coloured clothes, speaking Spanish; he was a Spanish gypsy. The point is that New Zealand is like the way every other place is now, but I was being surprised because it was unexpected, surprised in the way those early Tasmanians had been; it took time before they dared trust their own eyes.

Nevertheless, I have been to many places in the world, alone and minding my own business, and have never been so brazenly propositioned as in Auckland, nor forced to step off a path, in fear because of the look in a man's eyes, as in Wellington.

At the end of old Cuba Street, in the archives, it was the usual story. The file could not be found. Everyone was helpful, during a long morning, but no, it was not there. This was maddening, because I had the file number, it was noted in the card index as being there, and there was nowhere else it could be. Nearly defeated, I went in search of a pub and a sandwich, over which I could review the apparently hopeless situation. I had come a long way and I had found that the place was like every other place, apart from which I had found nothing – I could not even find a pub.

There were restaurants, but I did not want a restaurant, I wanted a pub and a sandwich, sulkily. I found a pub but it sold no food and it would only give me beer in a small glass. I wanted a large glass; there was a row of such glasses behind the barman's head, but he refused to fill one, as though dedicated to protecting me from alcoholism. So I drank the small glass and afterwards bought a salad sandwich from a small take-away, forced to eat it in the street. Then, at last, wiping lettuce from my chin, I spotted a dream-pub, magnificently Music Hall florid, Victorian, with its name, Royal Albion, in stone relief on its forehead. It might have been in Mortlake or Barnes, or some other comparatively unspoiled part of London. A place I could sit and think in while I planned my next move. Time was running out; I had arranged to fly to the South Island next day – not strictly part of my quest, so far as I knew no Kavanagh had set foot in the South Island but to hell with the Kavanaghs, this one would. I approached the Royal Albion with a lightened heart. The door was locked: an oddly discreet door, painted an unpublike colour, a sort of tasteful mulberry, and subliminal warning-signals sounded, not yet interpreted. There was a bell-push, and above the bell the one word, discreetly displayed: *Massage*.

The alternative to depression was rage and so, with a sense of making one last desperate charge, I strode grimly back to the archives. The staff might have changed, or come up with an idea, or *something*. Perhaps it was as well my gypsy acquaintance did not walk towards me as he had done earlier, or we might have walked through each other.

Vincent O'Sullivan, the poet, had given me the name of a friend of his in the archives, Ken Scadden (let his name be gratefully recorded), who had not been there in the morning. Now, with new-found belligerence, I demanded to see him, found him, and he invited me into his office. The amateur researcher, perhaps any sort of researcher, is in the position of a baby, demanding special treatment, because he is in a world he knows nothing about; the food is there, but he cannot reach it unless somebody unbuttons. Scadden heard out the problem, thought (how childishly grateful the researcher is to see an archivist think), rose from his desk ('Just a minute, I've an idea' – words above all others the suppliant wants to hear), vanished, and reappeared with the file.

Here, after many weeks, was a fat bundle of facts gathered together under one cover. After guesses and probablys and perhapses this was as great a luxury as the Royal Albion would have been if it was still a pub and not a massage parlour. In that file I was to discover aspects of my grandfather, and a respect for him, because of one part of his life that was possibly unknown even to his son. He was fifty-one when my father was born, so Henry Edward would have come to consciousness of his father, Henry Paul, when he was elderly, awesome and perhaps irritable.

The file is unsatisfactory in the sense that it only opens when Henry (as I soon felt able to call him) was already in his fifties. By then he had become a 'Crown Lands Ranger' and must have accumulated considerable experience before being given that job, if the Surveyor-General's description of it is anything to go by, when a successor was sought after Henry had been promoted:

> In filling the vacancy it is necessary to bear in mind that he shall be an active man in the prime of life, and a good bushman of sterling character and sober habits, possessed of a considerable amount of acumen, tact and firmness combined. . . . Of considerable farming knowledge and experience, both on bush and open lands: he should also have a good knowledge of the use of plans and tracings, and be able to make compass-surveys and valuations of the settlers' bush-felling and improvements. As the duties now performed by Mr Kavanagh necessitate all the above qualifications, it is necessary that his successor be a man of varied attainments and experience.

His job was to settle unemployed men on government land, which they would turn into farms, to check on their government-funded improvements and solve their disputes. It would have certainly demanded 'acumen, tact and firmness combined' to make sure that no one was encroaching on anybody else, or selling out to a land-speculator. For what above all the Ballance government, inspired by John McKenzie's memory of his evicted Highland father, wished to avoid, was too much land falling into too few hands. It was good to think of my grandfather being involved in work so decent, useful and tough. It must have involved long hours on horseback and, in his fifties, he could hardly have been 'in the prime of life.'

Salary £250 per annum. Travelling allowance 8/- per day to cover hotel expenses when away at night from his quarters, also coach, 'bus, stabling, & horse and trap hire on special occasions. Mr Kavanagh was allowed the services of a guide to take him through a Forestry Reserve he was inspecting.

His lonely beat (his wife and two sons seven hundred miles away in Auckland) was the Wairarapa in the Puketoi Range, roughly fifty miles from Wellington, among settlements with names like Makuri, Rakanui, Pongaroa. It was country that was uncleared in many places, as he says in his letter of thanks to the Wellington Land Board in 1905, when he had been posted back to Auckland ('When is Kavanagh coming?' cables impatient Auckland late in 1904): 'Although my transfer was in the way of promotion I desire to state that I left with feelings of regret the District in parts of which I have seen the lands converted from standing bush to smiling homesteads and dray roads, and I am sure that when I am sounding the depths of the mud in the roadless North I will be longing for the Woodville Railway and the Papa roads at Pongaroa.'

The South Island could wait. I had to inspect my grandfather's patrolling area, if only because here at last was something precisely defined. Scadden, the archivist, came from the Wairarapa and said it had barely changed this century. So I would be seeing what my grandfather saw at the end of his stint there, a landscape he had had a hand in creating.

I thought about that file early next morning, driving out of Wellington and along the Hutt river, as presumably Henry Paul had ridden, many times. The file threw a light back fifty years, to Van Diemen's Land. The respect in which my grandfather had been held, clear from his superiors' letters to each other, their trust in a man whose job must have given daily opportunities for favouritism and corruption, suggested that Patrick and Margaret had done a good job in the rearing of their children. Also, there had clearly been a decent education to be picked up at Father Butler's school in early, primitive Launceston.

Fish-hawks hovered above the river. There were rags of cloud over the dark hills, as though the hills smoked, and a black squall over the Heads, the entry to Wellington Harbour. I was to remember this later.

The hills were smooth but wrinkled, like the skin of a green elephant, or as though they were a plaster-relief map made by a too pedantic modeller. The clear light caught every fold and convexity. They had the appearance of smoothly grassed-over spoil-heaps, which in a sense is what they are, being volcanic. The sides of the steep Hutt Gorge were grown with delicate light-leaved bushes among darker ones, and this gave the wildness the appearance of a planned Victorian shrubbery. On the other side, in the plain, came grid-plan Masterton, a quiet place. I seemed to remember seeing an early letter by my medical-student father in which he expressed gloom at the thought of returning to practise medicine in Masterton, and I saw what he meant. His father did not live anywhere even as mildly populous as Masterton, but miles further along the road, at Pahiatura, nearer his patch of responsibility. Today that little township seems almost wholly given up to the sale of second-hand cars – they line the road there (perhaps, before, it was second-hand horses) – but the Reynold's Tavern is, I was told, a hundred years old, so he would have known that. Perhaps he even lived in it. It must have been a lonely life.

The loneliness of rural New Zealand, and that country's sometimes surreal attitude to the past, was made even more manifest when I was seduced by a roadside sign, not near any habitation, pointing towards 'The Bruce Mountain Folk Museum'. I followed where it pointed, along a track, myself followed by hopping white-backed magpies which seemed to have no fear of man, and came upon a hillside farm where the lone farmer – at least, no one else was about – stopped milking his real cows and, in silence, switched on a machine in a shed that mechanically milked a black-and-white mechanical cow. He sat on a milking-stool and watched my face while it did so. He followed me as I politely wandered round the shed looking at dusty horse-ploughs, old Ovaltine tins and metal advertisements for Virol. To what comments I could think of making he did not reply, but put a record on a wind-up gramophone and played an early monologue by an old-time English comedian, Sandy Powell, still attentively watching my face. Conceivably he was a little mad; I had no way of knowing, since it was my first rural contact in that place. Not quite the first, but the owner of the Reynold's Tavern had been no more communicative.

It was when I turned off the main road into my grandfather's district, towards Pongaroa, that I was hit for the first time by the full force of the picture-postcard, travel-poster overwhelming beauty of New Zealand. He must have traversed the place, up and down, hundreds of times, but of course he never mentioned its outstanding characteristic, tranquil beauty, mile after mile of it. It is an almost paradisal place. There are willows and poplars, probably imported; most of the native trees are dark and evergreen, in different tones and shades, which contrast with the brilliant emerald of the sometimes conical fields above them. These trees astonish in their variety of shape and tone. There are fir-like trees and yew-like trees, of great girth, and pohutokawa trees with grey bark, and palms, and lighter-coloured shrubs, like the tora; these are at the foot of the sheep-cropped, smooth and rounded, Irish-green pastures they give way to. It is the contrast between the various dark greens and the bright green fields that is exquisite, the perfect weedless turf on a succession of little ex-volcanoes; so perfect, that if it were not for the spectacular white of the sheep penned in corners, you might imagine the whole place, extending for dozens of miles, was an ingenious millionaire's golf course, with very short but glassily rippled fairways, and with tees and greens on mown plateaux and in moulded scoops. Even the sheep are exquisite, white, not grey, and of a particularly cuddly kind, Romneys, the sort that have curly fleece over their faces through which they peer. When you meet these on the road, being driven, you are not expected to wait but to point your car through them, and, unstartled, they mildly give way.

Occasionally, very occasionally, there is a white-painted 'smiling homestead', each one many miles from the next. My grandfather must have had access to all of these, and known the families in them. For him it may have been an isolated life but not a lonely one; although (I suppose) a kind of policeman, he was also there postively to help. It is good to think of him travelling those valleys and slopes, given their present beauty by the hand of man, for which soft loveliness the word now could be the Scottish 'douce', and of him having a hand in the clearing and settling and the justice of part of what is, after all, the point of New Zealand.

There are signs, however, that he felt the isolation. In 1899, from Pahiatura, he makes a formal Application for Removal (to Auckland) to the Commissioner of Crown Lands, giving his reasons:

My father is now eighty years of age and is failing, he wishes me to be nearer him.

I have two little boys aged eight and eleven years respectively and they require the presence and protection of their father, I feel I ought to be with them. Their grandmother lives with us and is seventy-eight years of age and growing feeble, she is too old to bring down here or to live by herself.

I further wish to point out that I find the double cost of maintaining a household in Auckland and living at hotel with my horse at livery here is more expensive than my salary permits of.

Please to notice also that I have been in this district for nearly *three and a half years* working under the said disability.

His masters take no notice, tell him they cannot replace him, so eventually he brings the family down anyway, by steamship, and puts them up in an hotel for a couple of months while he finds a house in Masterton, and sends the bill to the office. He does not get away with this act of impatience. 'To H. P. Kavanagh. Will you please attach to the enclosed voucher a memo explaining the circumstances which necessitated the payment of hotel expenses for your family for 6½ weeks, as it is unlikely that the audit department will pass this without some information.' He does explain, but the affair rumbles on until his boss sends a letter firm in his defence to the Surveyor-General, who pays up.

Did Carlow Patrick live in Auckland in Henry Paul's house, with my father, and then come to live in Masterton? The impression in Auckland was that he lived with his daughter, in Te Makiri. Perhaps he did both. So Patrick was eighty years old in 1899? That means he was definitely twenty-three when he left Carlow. So his son, Henry Paul, lived 'at hotel' in Pahiatura? It must have been the Reynold's Tavern, which still has a sign on its wall suggesting that it once was a hotel; the place is too small to have two.

At all events, he settled his numerous dependants in

Masterton, this upright and responsible man, in reasonable style. This last is known because, as is the way of things, no sooner had he found and furnished a house than he was granted his wish and promoted to Auckland. He had to sell up and the auctioneer's advertisement proudly mentions, among other glories, in the sale contents, 'A Splendid Upright Grand Piano [*sic*] by Esdail and Co., London. Ebony and Gold case . . .'. This would be for my grandmother, Jane, whose scores of Schubert and Beethoven were found, mildewed, in the basement of St Mary's Road in the 1980s, together with, intriguingly, a collection of my grandfather's (great-grand-father's?) 'Irish genealogical books'.

Why had my father never mentioned to me that he had shared a house with his Irish grandfather? He would have done so when he was nine years old, at least, and would have surely remembered him. He never did mention Patrick, so far as I recall, and only two or three times mentioned his father. Do parents usually mention their grandparents to their children? Perhaps not. Or perhaps his sense of break in continuity was too great, or he disbelieved in continuity altogether. Indeed, a continuity is hard to establish. Nevertheless, I began to feel that something somewhere had gone wrong.

A little drunk with the perfection of the Wairarapa, I drove back to Masterton and was faced, thirsty, with the usual embarrassment of wandering like a wino in search of a glass of beer, failing to find one. I was staying at a motel, and they are not usually places to sit in and mope, or to find beer. Unable to spot an Irish face (there were not many faces about), I asked the first promising beer-belly where I could get a drink in Masterton. He jerked back a little, as though fearful of my alcoholic breath (I had been driving and map-reading and exploring and trying to imagine, for about eight hours) or as though I was going to touch him for the price of one, but he relented, and laughed. 'Well, I've been fifty-eight years in Masterton, and I've never asked myself that question. I drink it

Patrick Kavanagh c. 1900

at home.' I could see why my sociable father dreaded living here. However, he pointed out a sign, almost invisible, and told me I should climb the stairs and I would find a drink.

I did so, later, and instead of a pub found one of those places that are only now appearing in England, where you serve yourself from a multitude of bowls and platters, and where there is a bar. It was crowded with other eaters and drinkers who had somehow found their way there along what had seemed to me almost empty streets. I was as far as ever from understanding how life works in the Antipodes. It never failed to surprise me. Early next morning I wrote a piece for a magazine which I intended to post when I returned to Wellington – Masterton is, it has to be said again, a quiet and old-fashioned place – but there I stumbled across a shining new office in the main street which contained the latest fax machine and the article was on the editor's desk within a minute and a quarter. That was the second surprise in Masterton, and I was about to receive a third, a reminder of how tough my grandfather's life must sometimes have been.

17

Henry Edward

On the day before, there had been those rags of low cloud in the hills, and a black squall over the sea, but in Masterton, safely the other side of the Rimutaka Range, the sky had been merely mild and grey. Further on, among the low hills of the Wairarapa, this greyness had given lustre to the colours of 'the bush', the dark evergreens and the close-cropped conical pastures, and made the fawn backs of kestrels, Australian harriers, glow.

I had noticed coming over the pass that the sides of it had a sub-tropical Grand Hotel shrubbery look, and now, climbing it again from the other side, these pretty shrubs were dancing about; a wind had sprung up. Further up, they began to detach themselves, roots and all, and do their dance at speed across the road. It was when rocks the size of cricket balls began to rattle down the steep sides of the gorge, one of them hitting the car, that I noticed mine was the only car on the pass; it was a lightweight, and became difficult to control.

Round a bend there suddenly was another car, slewed across the road, stopped, and a second one, also stationary, with its wheels dangerously near the precipice edge. They had obviously blown into each other. There was a girl in the car that blocked the road and she appeared to be doing nothing, just sitting as though in shock, as were the two young men in the other car. In the time it took to take this in a small queue formed behind me of vehicles ascending, and out of a lorry, apparently without hesitation, jumped a burly middle-aged man in blue overalls, white hair streaming in the wind. He staggered head down to the car on the edge and somehow encouraged the young men to continue on down. Then he turned his attention to the crosswise car, tried to walk towards it, staggered again, fell, and began slowly to be blown across the road, saving himself by wrapping his arms round one of the wind-shaken posts that marked the edge. He waited, head pressed to the ground, for the gust to expend itself, and then this apotheosis of Australasian mateyness crawled on his belly towards the girl's car, clutched it, levered himself up by the doorhandle, made her wind down her window and, sticking his head inside, talked to her, shouting to make himself heard above the great noise of the wind. In the driving-mirror I could see a heavy red Mercedes behind me, with six people it it, rocking and bouncing. The bonnet of my little Toyota was bending with the gusts, as though thinking about take-off, and I reckoned if I got out, hoping to help, it might blow away altogether. Meanwhile the lorry-driver had pushed the girl's car to the lee of the mountain, a descending lorry-driver was calling for help on his cab radio – she was either too damaged or too shaken to drive – and we were waved on up, I in the lead and wishing I was not. However, we got up, and then down, with only minor damage from blown rocks, and down on the plain the water of the Hutt river was rising in spirals, the sea invisible under black spray.

It was only a slap on the wrist, but it reminded me how little I knew about what it was like to live in New Zealand, or could know, unless I made a longer, different kind of journey. My job was to keep the focus narrow, to clarify as far as I could the story of one family, which would perhaps suggest a larger picture. The aim was modest and possible, and enclosed me, as did the spume from the sea that raged at the side of the road, and the black clouds, that day, which enclosed most of the North Island. There were no flights in such weather from

Wellington to the South Island, so I had decided to drive the seven hundred miles back to Auckland.

As I drove, through nearly invisible New Zealand, I tried to put into order what I thought I had found so far. The force of the nationalist-Irish-Catholic feeling which must have affected my great-grandfather, not least because of his Cullen connections: Patrick had passed this on to Henry Paul: Henry Paul had been pro-Boer, anti-imperial (my father had been told by his mother), and his devout church benefactions must have mostly been to Irish priests and nuns – 'Ponsonby was full of the Irish in those days'. Henry Paul passed these views on to his son, my father, who as a medical student in Edinburgh wanted to go over to Dublin during the Easter Rising to give what medical help he could (I was told by *my* mother), and this was the air I breathed as a boy. I had no reason to be puzzled by it or wonder if I had made it up. It was an inheritance, and potent enough. My father left me nothing else (he had, at the end, nothing else to leave). Just as his father had left nothing else to him.

But why was that, when Henry Paul died apparently cluttered with possessions and, I had been told, with money? The answer must lie in Auckland, where he died, and where his wife died shortly after him.

There was little to remember from that dark drive, except the taste of a New Zealand apple bought at the roadside, like no apple tasted since boyhood. In it lay the sweetness of New Zealand, why people had come here in the first place. Sometimes the clouds parted, and some of that rural sweetness was revealed, but my focus was on Auckland.

There I wandered again along Ponsonby Road, Richmond Road where my father's school had been, St Mary's Road where he had lived with his parents in the larger house and where, when their sons left home, his parents had moved to a smaller one a few doors away. Again I tried to see what they had seen, tried to enter their lives, even by an inch; again I felt the warning, as though on a path that might lead to the betrayal of my father; but I knew I would have no part in that. But persistence paid. Letters from my father, even a telegram, surfaced; they had been preserved by his brother, and in them it seems as though the brothers were almost forced to become conspirators.

The past is easy enough to betray, by over-simplification, by ignorance, but an attempt can be made to give it sequence. Patrick came to Australia and survived, in whatever way. The early question – why did he leave Ireland – seemed to be answered on every hand: Why not? With 39 per cent of its population living outside it by 1890 he must have belonged to the majority, of those capable of leaving it at all: three million of them, reinventing 'the Old Sod' in their imaginations. In New Zealand his son, by hard work, had finished up Chief Timber Expert for the Crown Lands Department, a respected citizen, as far as a Catholic of Irish descent could be. 'Ten per cent of the population. . . . The faith was kept alive by people like your grandfather.' He had married into the Catholic and, Simmons had told me, the influential Lorigan family. Perhaps his wife had resources of her own. 'Jane Kavanagh more or less built that place,' said Diane Wilson, staring up at the Mercy Hospital. The extent of the benefactions of the Kavanaghs is still a source of puzzlement to their surviving connections.

My mother (not a reliable witness – no one is when they talk of the past, of people they never met) told me that grandfather Henry Paul left everything to his wife Jane, having more or less cut off his sons, and Jane was going to change this, help my father Eddie and his family in London, but she fell ill, her deathbed was surrounded by priests, and the church got everything.

Maybe. My mother's Catholicism did not include a generalised affection for priests. There was perhaps more to the story than that.

My father's brother Paul became a barrister. He was set up

in his own firm, Kavanagh, de Coek & Boylan, by his father, but there was some trouble with the use of money, not the firm's own, and Paul was debarred from practising in the courts. The other son, Henry Edward – Eddie in New Zealand, Ted in England, my father – was training to be a doctor in Scotland, out of sight. Medicine and the Law for his two sons: the dream of many fathers, passport to the nearest New Zealand could allow as an aristocracy, to a rich marriage (my father hints as much in one of his letters), dynastic justification for Patrick's voyage from Carlow seventy years before, and reward for those hard solitary years in the Wairarapa; but before Henry's death there was one son debarred, and the other had dropped out of medicine.

Perhaps my father never wanted to be a doctor. His training in Edinburgh was interrupted by the First World War; he joined up, and after that he married. My mother used to describe how pleased she was to see him 'getting down to his books' and then she would find that inside *Gray's Anatomy*, or whatever, there had been a novel hidden. He always doctored us when we were children; he would have made a good paediatrician.

But I was surprised to learn the extent of the pain of it all, and understood why I had felt warned off. I was more than surprised to discover that my father, that genial, rock-like figure of my childhood memory, had been so frightened of his own father, and guilty about the disappointment he had caused, that as late as 1926, seven years married, he had not yet dared to tell his parents about this marriage, nor that he had a five-year-old son, my brother, and had given up medicine. His letter to his brother Paul (whom he clearly had not told either) was written from London when Henry Paul fell ill in Auckland, aged about eighty-one. My father was already thirty-four.

My dear Paul,
    Your cable has spurred me on to write you a long-

promised letter, often started but never finished. The cable
was rather a shock to me, all reports from Mother were good
– Father very active etc. but, of course, his age renders even
the slightest upset serious for him. I am sure he has the best
attention – I don't suppose Maskell is much use but you will
know who knows the most, especially about diabetes. I
imagined that I would have to leave London immediately,
hence my cable, but so far have heard no further. I can of
course leave here at anytime but unless my fare appears in
some miraculous manner, I see little hope of seeing
Auckland again for some years. In many ways I rather dread
going home. Naturally I am keen on seeing you all again, it is
a constant nightmare to me that either Mother or Father
should die before I get back, but I know that not only from
home, but from everyone I meet, I shall have to face a perfect
inquisition and that I shall be regarded as an utter failure.
Personally, I don't think I'm a failure at all. I am quite
capable of earning my own living here or in practically any
English-speaking country with the possible exception of
N.Z. – my services are in great demand in London as a
medical journalist. I had not realised its scope until recently
and am seeing new opportunities every day. When I
received your cable I told Burroughs Wellcome & Co who
had an option on my services that I would possibly have to
leave for N.Z. and they offered to keep a position open for me
– a considerable tribute from a firm of their calibre, and an
international organisation. Only one thing handicapped me
and that is rotten health. I look forward to the long trip home
(not *Home*) to put me on my feet again. I'm supposed at
present to have a bad heart. I have had one or two syncope
attacks which put the wind up me and everyone around but,
thank God, feel a bit better now. I didn't say much about it
in my letters home as I didn't want to upset them, but for
some time past I have been quite unfit to sit exams. I never
could do myself justice and repeated failure has knocked my

nerves and self-confidence all to hell. However, I think I am better – a good rest and freedom from anxiety would make me quite well I am certain. I don't think there's anything organically wrong – only functional. Four years ago when assisting a doctor during vacation I drank out of a measuring-glass in which the dispenser had evidently left a lot of strychnine. Within a few minutes I had all the pains and spasms of acute strychnine poisoning and really felt I had commenced my ascent to the next world (at least it felt like an ascent but I may have been deceived by the strychnine!). Anyhow, I nearly died. Only for prompt remedial measures I would have ceased to be! I have felt the ill-effects ever since. I feel I simply couldn't face general practice – if I did qualify I should probably get a hospital or asylum job – or even the Editorship of a medical paper would be worth considering. I felt it was exceedingly good of you to have cabled and whatever happens I know I can leave my affairs safe in your hands. My sojourn here must have sadly depleted the family funds and I have no 'expectations' in that direction at all. I am so used to being hard-up that money has no great use or fascination for me. I have no doubt that had I qualified in good time Father would have set me up in practice, but I have no hope of anything like that now. Father has always sent my draft with great generosity and regularity but, of course, cost of living here is 75% higher than in 1914 – my allowance is almost 50% less than in that year – you can draw your own conclusions. Recently I have written home and told them I can keep myself quite well – I really haven't the face to keep on taking money from home any longer. You seem to have heard that I am married – you can take it from me it is quite official. It is about the most successful thing I have done except in one way. I have never felt in a position to tell them at home and this has led me into such constant evasion and such subterfuge in all my letters home that I feel quite sick when I think of it. Only for this I would have written more often. You must know that you have never been quite forgiven for your matrimonial 'lapse' and even after all these years, though Mother's letters are full of praise for Buster and they are pleased with your success on 'The Month', occasionally there peeps through just a hint of old grievance. I can't understand how good people, pious and obedient to the Church in everything can be so obdurate – when priests are everywhere and always declaiming against late marriage, mixed marriage or no marriage at all. What possible objection can there be to anyone who marries a Catholic girl in a Catholic church as you did and I did I can't imagine, except perhaps economic reasons – purely worldly. I always felt that once I was qualified I could tell them at home with impunity, but, otherwise, considering Father's age and his choleric disposition, a sudden upset and consequent outburst might have killed him and then I, and incidentally all belonging to me, would be blamed. I have suffered enough as it is without that but you can understand that my peace of mind has suffered too. I often considered telling Mother, but then, wouldn't she feel compelled to pass it on? You will be the best judge, as to whether you should 'break the news' – as if it were the one unforgiveable crime. It reads just like when the heir to the Dukedom marries the barmaid from the Bodega. Well, I didn't marry a barmaid or anyone connected with the 'Trade'. I was married in Glasgow in 1919 and have had two kids, one of whom died suddenly from meningitis when ten months old – a terrible blow, he was so bright and getting on so well. The other whom we called Kevin Paul is now nearly six. He has got on well and been a great consolation to us as well as providing great amusement. He is always very keen to know all about Buster (whom, by the way, he calls his nephew). I will send you a photo as soon as I get one. I was terribly sorry to hear that you and Wyn had lost your second baby – there is no explanation apparently of hydramnios, some say it is pressure in the kidneys, or too high blood pressure, but as in most things they really don't know. It was a hard knock for you both. I suppose Buster is quite big now, he must be nearly eleven. I am longing to see him and getting him to show me round new Auckland. I could easily leave the family in good hands here and come home but of course I would have to come back at least for a short time. After receiving your cable I thought I would receive the fare and leave at once, and have left this letter open till near mail-time but have heard no further. I hope I can get home again in time to see and make my peace with Father. Fr Martindale and Father Warde are saying Mass for my intention. I am longing to see you all again, though I dread returning home in the circumstances. Give my love to Wyn and Buster (or is he too big to be called Buster now?) and to all at the Shore. I have written this in rather a hurry, but having broken the ice will write by next mail as I have a lot to write about,

your loving brother
Eddie.

There is a further letter, almost as revealing, written a month later.

My dear Paul,

This is a rather hurried letter as I have just found at the G.P.O. that there is a Mail at 2 a.m. – it is now 12 a.m. Your cable reached me at Burroughs Wellcome but bore no name so was slightly delayed. I was relieved to get it, but will feel rather worried as to what my 'fare' will consist of. I am quite willing to travel steerage, would welcome it in fact, but I can't leave London with my bare fare and my small family unprovided for. Yet, by the time this reaches you all will probably be settled. The various cables have led me into a good deal of expense. Naturally I took your first cable to mean that haste was all-important. I gave notice all round and left myself quite free to sail at once, only to find no fare forthcoming and a new series of complications regarding qualifying in N.Z. In common honesty I could not promise to qualify anywhere Father wanted at the present moment. I dread the very mention of Medicine. My only hope of regaining decent health is to leave it entirely alone for the present. Again, I would need at least two years or more at Dunedin and then probably into General Practice in N.Z., a thing I could not face. It is enough of an ordeal to go back to Auckland unqualified! This worry and uncertainty has made me a bit shaky. I'm supposed to have a touch of goitre but probably a trip and a rest will cure that – it chokes me now and again but is not really dangerous.

You have your share of worries I'm sure. You must have difficulty with father over my return – I do wish I could give him some little return during his life for all he has done for me. Mother seems bright, but perhaps her letters are deceptively lively. I hear Wyn is to welcome another stranger in November, this time with great ease and exuberance I'm sure. Be certain your doctor pays frequent visits and leaves nothing to chance. Bi-weekly urinalysis and careful examination especially in the last few weeks will prevent all mishaps. There I am, off into medicine again against the doctor's orders! Will write again before leaving. Fr Martindale is saying mass for Father and all of us, also other clerical friends. May their prayers be heard!

> your loving brother
> Eddie

Paul appears to have kept everything sent him by his brother, including that telegram, six years later, which I wish I had not seen. So, possibly, these are the only letters my father wrote to him.

I hesitated before including them here, but did so in the end because, if anything, they make me even fonder of my father than I was before. The desperate sound of a man (nearly) trapped in the wrong profession is touching and appealing; an intelligent man's inability to make a go of the world is attractive, to me. Although perhaps I might have felt differently if the story did not have, in a sense, a happy outcome; he did make a go of it in the end, on his own, not on his father's, terms.

Within a few years of the dispatch of those letters – or, at least, the sending of the telegram – he was helping to make the whole of Britain laugh, together, in greater numbers than it ever had before. Circumstances helped him – wartime, blackout, lack of petrol, people trapped at home with a new toy, radio, needing to be made to laugh. It was also a team effort, as all such programmes are. But it was his pen which wrote the words of *Itma* (I saw it doing so in Bristol, firemen playing their hoses against the outside wall of our flat, the next-door house having been burnt out by incendiary bombs), in Wales, in London, and the writing was the same as in the letters found in Auckland; he had not changed. As the number of people who remember that programme, last broadcast in 1948, must be diminishing fast, it is worth recording this before all memory of it fades, and memory of him.

There is much that is odd in those letters. The talk of his ill-health is strange, from a man who always boasted to me that he had never had a day's illness in his life, nor did he while I knew him. It is true that he never cared for money. When he had any he usually gave it away. Perhaps it is the classic case of a father, Henry Paul, struggling to accumulate, and siring sons whose passion is dispersal. His older son Paul's genial weakness was 'the horses', which left him permanently short of funds, but when he had money he too, I was told, was fond of giving people treats. Paul must have regretted having to preside over the donation of his father's Maori collection to the museum, in St Mary's Road, after his father's death; he signed the

Ted Kavanagh in mid-1950s

inventory. Even then, in 1925, it was valued at many thousands of pounds. It is easy to imagine his face set in an expression of resigned farewell as he saw it all carted away, when just one carved *tiki*, or greenstone axe-head, placed, as it were, on the nose of a horse, might have solved his problems for ever.

The mystery of the non-arrival of the fare to New Zealand must remain one. Presumably it did not come, because my father worked his passage as ship's purser, and he arrived in time to see his father alive. That the troubles in England did not decrease is shown in the last piece of paper preserved in New Zealand, a cry of utter desperation. It is dated 26 August 1931. I had been born seven months before, eleven years after my surviving brother, at the heart of the Depression; economically I cannot have been welcome:

IMPOSSIBLE HOLD OUT LONGER IMPLORE HELP FUTURE PROSPECTS RUINED FAILING IMMEDIATE REPLY
EDDIE

18

Fathers and Sons

Perhaps Henry Paul did not believe in inheritance; my father did not. Perhaps his work in the Wairarapa, settling the unemployed on small farms of their own, made him dislike the idea of large owners of anything by inheritance.

Apart from the obvious reasons for unease in my father's letters – his previous and long-standing failure in frankness, his lack of anything to boast home about, his simultaneous claim that he expects no financial help from home and confession of how hard-pressed he is – there is an underlying discomfort of tone, as though he did not know his brother well. This would be likely. Paul was four years older, born in 1888, and because of his father's connection with Wellington, at least from the 1890s on, was educated there and at Wellington University, whereas my father went to school and university in Auckland.

What at least is clear is that Henry Paul despaired of his two sons (if he did so) too soon, as fathers tend to. Whatever went on at Kavanagh, de Coek & Boylan, and whether Paul was to blame or another member of the firm (stories differ in Auckland), it cannot have been grave, or too disgraceful, because for the next thirty years he was the editor of the *New Zealand Law Journal*, and of other official and semi-official legal reports. On his retirement the *Law Journal* is fulsome: 'It is not too much to query whether his work has been equalled in excellence of editorship and facility of style and diction, by any legal journalist of the British Commonwealth.' Henry Paul could have been proud of him.

As for his other son, my father, he was as generous with his time and money to Catholic causes as his father had been: to the Catholic Stage Guild, the Catholic Writers' Guild, and so on. If his father was the kind of man he hints he was in his letters, he would have been proud that his son was knighted for this by the Pope. (Before my father's funeral we were asked by the priest whether he would have liked a cocked hat and sword on top of the coffin when it was lying in the church, and we had difficulty in remaining serious, because nothing could have been less appropriate. He had earned his living, made his name, by deflating all forms of self-importance.)

Where did his particular form of humour come from, that had a touch of the surreal about it, original at the time, absorbed and developed in comedy since? In Auckland, surrounded by the atmosphere of New Zealand which is not in itself lighthearted, surrounded also by thoughts, notes and readings about the Irish influence in Australasia, I had no difficulty in believing that it came from there, and perhaps from an unconscious desire to tease his father; that it came from a sense that the kind of temperament fostered and most sucessful in his birthplace needed teasing – 'If we have bettered ourselves, what then?' – and that it came from New Zealand by way of dissident Ireland, which so much values word-play. Its basis was a suspicion of all secular authority, a need to highlight the absurdity of authority's claims to have more than the most superficial control over what we think and feel. That suspicion, in different ways, is in the air of Australasia and of Ireland. Surely, also, it was connected with his deep-seated troubles with the authority of his elderly father, and the way it had tried, and failed, to give a conventional direction to his life.

About the time he was writing those apparently agonised letters he was fiddling with the cat's whisker of his crystal wireless set, when doubtless he should have been reading his medical books or trying to earn some money. One day he caught the comic patter of a comedian whose voice amused him, so he wrote him a sketch: 'Eddie's patter, as a boy, is still remembered' (or nearly remembered) by that correspondent in New Zealand. He sent it in and heard no more. Then, fiddling again, he heard the comedian broadcasting the sketch, so he set off in search of the man, and the fee. Thus began his long association with the comedian Tommy Handley, culminating in *Itma*, which made Handley one of the most famous comedians in the world, and my father solvent.

The strange thing about *Itma* is that everybody in it is bent, in the sense of crooked, on the make in an amiable and hopeless way. Their aim is to evade authority in any form ('The Ministry of Twerps') by creating their own, upside-down, version of it. Handley is usually the mayor (that English type of empty authority) of some such seaside resort as Foaming-at-the-Mouth, or he is the squire of Much Fiddling (perhaps the type Henry Paul had no wish to see rising in the Wairarapa). He is an authority figurehead but the opposite of authoritarian, full of absurd schemes which are constantly thwarted by the sudden, unexplained appearance, and equally sudden disappearance, of surreal figures: Ali Oop, trying to sell him saucy postcards; a deep-sea diver who asks for money – 'Every penny makes the water warmer' – and exits to the sound of bubbles; a nervous Chicago gangster, Sam Scram, who cannot shoot straight, or at all – 'It's me noives, boss, it's me noives!' Word-play, patter; Bessie Braddock, MP, scornfully called the programme 'a welter of bad puns', to my father's delight. It was like a better class of dream.

On the day *The Times* published my father's obituary in 1958, it also printed a Fourth Leader on the subject of *Itma*. This article attempted to turn the programme into an expression of 'the British power to infuse gallantry with gaiety'. (It incidentally contains an astonishing statistic: 'at one time its three listening audiences during each week added up to over 100% of the adult population.') 'The ancestors of *Itma*'s characters', says *The Times*, 'went back far beyond Shakespeare's clowns . . . were at Hastings, Crécy, Agincourt.' In the last few lines *The Times* really gets into that sort of stride: 'Now TOMMY HANDLEY, FRANCIS WORSLEY and TED KAVANAGH (Lancashireman, Yorkshireman and New Zealander), the three inseparables without any of whom *Itma* would not have been the potent and high-spirited manifestation of national character it was, are all gone. Happily by the time they set to work recording had been brought to perfection. Future historians, when they come to examine the documents and archives of Britain's stern and glorious years, will be wise to listen to *Itma* if they want to know what kind of people we really were.'

Well – maybe; the writer is doing his best to praise, in English terms. But it was that side of England, that *tone* of England, more than a little pleased with itself, that my father most made fun of. He was a patriot, of course, but he was also a man whose grandfather had been close to the priest who helped John Mitchel escape; his father had been in trouble for his anti-imperialism, his opposition to the Boer War; he had himself wanted to go to help medically during the Easter Rising in Dublin. As far as his contribution to the triumvirate was concerned, I feel it derived more from his Irish-colonial-Roman Catholic background than from the spirit of Crécy and Agincourt, at which his ancestors were unlikely to have been present, unless kerns and gallowglasses were there. They came from a different island, from a race that has always raised its eyebrows (at least) at the sonorities of English self-congratulation. His gift was peculiar. It was not, I think, British pride of race disguised as jokes. It would be good to rescue him from that sort of approval, because I saw him shrug it away when he was alive. (Which is not to say that he would not have liked some sort of 'honour' after the war. I was surprised when I guessed this; but he contained contradiction, like everyone. That no 'honour' was awarded shows good Establishment instinct; by temperament, gift and history he was outside it.)

At the risk of making him raise his eyebrows again at the suggestion, I believe his humour was based on his tragic sense of life. A character in William Faulkner asks God why he created the suffering world, and God replies, 'Between grief and nothing, I chose grief.' As a response to such a world it is not unreasonable for a man to choose humour.

After Sally died in 1958, and shortly before his own death, he took me out to lunch, embarrassed as he always was by the prospect of having to be 'fatherly'. 'Now that something terrible has happened to you,' he said, humbly, 'perhaps you'll write comedy?'

I knew this was far from the 'Laugh, clown, laugh!' commonplace it might sound. Humour can be evasion; Edward Thomas called it 'that monkey, humour' and praised Richard Jefferies for his lack of it, but it can also be the response of a man who knows that life is far too serious to be taken, in public, other than lightly.

In his private life there was religion, and more good works than I knew. When in funds he was inclined to be a dandy, fond of good clothes, as I am. He bought his hats from a shop in Bond Street, and shortly after he died I went there to buy a hat for myself. After I handed over the cheque an elderly assistant came from the back of the shop, having noticed the name, and asked me if Ted was my father. He took me aside and said quietly, 'Your father has helped more people in need than anyone will ever know.' My brother found his desk was stuffed with old IOUs from friends and acquaintances, many for considerable sums which, even when his money ran out, he never called in.

He managed to reach New Zealand in time to say goodbye to his father in 1926, but never saw his brother after that, and I doubt if he even wrote; the part in us that cherishes the past was missing in him, or maybe suppressed. My brother wrote to Paul when Ted died in 1958 and received an affectionate letter back. In 1966 my brother died, the letter somehow passed to me, and I kept it, perhaps even then half conscious that I might one day have to go on some sort of rummage in the past, which my father had left nearly a blank.

In one place Paul's letter from New Zealand, inevitably, plays over the old Irish themes:

The Governor-General asked me, when I was at a party in Government House, if I was related to Dermot McMurrough Kavanagh. He was grandson of Arthur, and my father often wrote to his brother, the head of the Carlow family to which we all belong, mostly about horses and breeding. Our grandfather (Patrick) was a real old Irish gentleman of the old school, and he came from the estate though the 'heads' were not Catholics but very loyal to Ireland. Incidentally, my grandfather wanted to marry a Miss Paul, but her parents had more cows than his people, and the marriage was frowned on. She wrote, and told her uncle, Cardinal Cullen. He must have been a good old sport, because he sent her the money to elope to Dublin, where he would marry them. 'And then', he said, 'no one can say a word about your marriage since the Primate of All Ireland has tied the knot.' She was, of course, Msgr. Paul's sister. (Her great-grandmother had the unique distinction in the Church of having both a son and a grandson Cardinals. The other was Cardinal Moran, of Sydney, whom we met when we were boys, and he wanted us to visit him as his guest in Sydney.)

Paul must have known Patrick, for he was nineteen when Patrick died; known and talked to the man who had more or less eluded me across two islands on the other side of the world, as well as in Carlow. I could have asked Paul about him, if I had woken up earlier I could have asked my father, and Paul's single descriptive phrase is not helpful.

'Her people had more cows than his people': that, too, is perhaps just a phrase, but how entrenched is the rural, simple-folk image, the idyll of Erin, in the imaginations of expatriates of Irish descent. Her people were urban industrialists, maltsters; cows would not have been their concern. I only know this because I went to look, and the trouble with looking is that nearly all the old stories collapse and few new ones take their place. Patrick and Margaret were married in Carlow, not Dublin, and Father Cullen was in Rome at the time. He did not become Archbishop of Armagh until 1849, when they were both in Van Diemen's Land, and was made Cardinal, 'Primate of All Ireland', in 1866, the year Patrick and Margaret decamped to New Zealand with their large family which contained, among others, Paul's own grown-up father . . .

How did he, barrister, editor, student of racing form, pass on this hearsay as truth when a glance at a reference book would have shown him it was impossible? At times you can doubt whether anything at all you are told about the past is *true*. Shortly before he died my brother told me he had been 'finding out about the family' and when I asked him what he had found he told me to find out for myself. This was not as bad as it sounds. We were close (unlike – possibly – Paul and Ted), but he was eleven years older and fond of pointing out to his younger brother the realities of the present – life should not be made too easy for poncy poets, get some service in, and so on. All very salutary; but I have now spent so long discovering the *un*realities of the past, as it presented itself to us, that I wonder if what he found out was true. Our interest in the family is an Irish trait, I learn; my father must have been an exception. Mayhew was surprised to discover, among the poor in London, how unusually clear the Irish were about their origins. Let us hope they had some of the facts right.

19
Yes 'Home'

The present can be looked at and interpreted with more confidence than the past, it is under your nose. It was time I went back to it – (Yes *Home*). On the early-morning Air New Zealand flight to Sydney the omelette was good and I told the steward so. In England the response would be (and it was what I now expected), 'Thank you, sir. Glad you enjoyed it.' Polite, but keeping the social distance, or role distance, intact. In England you can forget how constricting and unnatural these separations still remain. This steward was interested; he had noticed the omelettes too. 'Yes, I thought it looked good. Sort of moist inside, wasn't it. Thanks, I'll tell the cook.' This naturalness is what has happened to New Zealand and Australia (it is also, and I harp on it, what you find in Ireland), it is what those places still have to teach us, and there are signs some of us are learning: that we do not need an elaborate system of social boundaries, defined hierarchies, in order to make a society safe to live in; we can manage with less authority, not more. Perhaps it is in bewilderment at the lack of such a need (still second nature for many older Englishmen, and infectious; I had found myself stratifying and classifying those men in the Melbourne pub, by their haircuts, before I had even noticed how small was my glass of beer) – perhaps it is this genuine absence of class-consciousness, that makes the English think of Australians as rude and rough. Rough they can be – that pub like the Klondyke in the Western Tiers, at Moina, and the Saturday night crowd at the Royal Oak in

Launceston (even the thought of which could make the Indian hotel manager, who loved Tasmania, wince) – they can relax together to the point of dissolution, but in their exchanges with each other they are more intimate but more carefully polite than we are in England. My grandfather had helped to create this sense of equality, it had been part of his job. My father had brought the sense of it with him to London, it is in his comedy. Where, therefore, do I stand on the subject of Class and Authority, who am shaped by England?

This, I realised, on the first leg of my journey home, was the question I had started from, standing in front of the Croppie Grave. There my inbred sympathy had been as great as ever, for these were the dispossessed, the untimely dead. Then I had wondered whether authority could have behaved otherwise, or had only been doing its job.

This had been a new thought for me to treat hospitably, and I had wondered if I had turned my tweed coat. Because I had always felt ill at ease with authority – 'wild Irishman at school' – most of all when I agreed with it. Those who took the side of authority when young I had always considered prematurely middle-aged. Now I was middle-aged, what did I think? Someone has said that England spent four centuries trying to teach Ireland to grow up. I was glad England had failed, if he meant what I think he did, but was it an absurd attempt at youthfulness of the heart that still made me approach all things from an odd angle, quirkily, that impelled me to take a path different from accepted, authoritative ones? What was I up to? Was an Irish gene responsible, or an irresponsible Irish dream? *Why were we such pests?*

The absence of class-imposed authority had been evident at once in Melbourne on Anzac Day. The Australasians had rid themselves of it, my father had made fun of it and of almost every other kind of authority. You could, I suppose, say that 'a welter of bad puns' even mocks the authority of language itself. My attitude had been shaped by him more than I would have liked. For how could I, as a son, have defined myself by reacting against the authority of a father who did not believe in authority, or class? This was a deprivation, because we define ourselves by such early reaction, and I had had nothing, or not much, to react against.

Yet some form of authority is necessary, and he had submitted himself to the most authoritarian government of all, that of the Church, with its hierarchies and dogmas and ceremonies. (I remembered the shudder I had felt in Auckland, noticing the pathos and tawdriness of the vestments laid out in the library, and the sudden doubt that it was all a sham. For I too had accepted the authority of the Church; up to a point, but it was around that point my life was gathered.)

All along, when using the word 'Catholic' I have often meant Christian, for it is Christianity that matters, not Popes; but can Christianity survive, be catholic, without the authority of supranational hierarchies? The Church of England, for all its beauties and gentlenesses, is not an encouraging example, because, being national, it has an inevitable class tinge about it, at least in England; there is this tinge, of other classes, in the chapels: the strata of class as it were Christianised. Whereas Catholicism transcends class and nation, or should do. How subtle Cullen and his associates were to make a connection (up to a point) between being a Catholic and a sense of being Irish, the last reinforcing the first, to allow (encourage) a sense of internal separation from a hated government, thus combining, for a larger purpose, the human needs to belong and to disagree.

But only up to a point: Cullen was against revolution, rebellion, Fenianism. That is why, until recently, he has had a bad press: Irish nationalists cannot claim him as their own. The Irish historian, R. F. Foster, is a recent reappraiser: 'The broader picture shows his constant efforts to sustain Irish Roman Catholicism as a national church while tirelessly monitoring it for signs of secular impropriety . . . and he was preoccupied with the dangers of revolutionary anarchism and nihilism: Continental examples were inescapably vivid to a hierarchy so closely connected to Rome. But anti-Fenianism did not imply anti-nationalism. Cullen simply took a different path.'

Not so simply, perhaps: Father Butler, from Kilkenny, helped John Mitchel to escape from Van Diemen's Land; also another Young Irelander, Terence Bellew McManus, allowing authority to arrest the wrong man. The political ambivalences of the Irish church baffle everybody outside it. No wonder the British authorities found the Irish, and Catholics in general, a pest.

But I like Foster's phrase about Cullen – that he 'took a different path.' Why should I not do that? Why not reject the over-clarifications of authority, which make us cut each other's throats: believe and not believe in all sorts of only apparently contradictory things so long as I believed in one large thing, as did the simpleton and the barmaid in Trim, which left them a part of a still cohesive whole?

I knew now how that large idea had come to me. It came, in its international form, from Ireland, through Patrick and Margaret, through Henry Paul and Jane, people I never met, and through my parents. I have pushed and pulled at the idea, tested it, neglected it, attempted to forget it altogether, but it has always held because it gives significance to our lives, opens them out endlessly, as well as being hard and clear in shape. I have tried to pass it on to my children although, child of my generation, I could not do this through authority. If it is an idea worth having it cannot depend on my imposition of it. Yet Cullen, and Butler, believed it was a matter of education, of the transmission by authority of accumulated wisdom. Spirituality left to itself rapidly becomes eccentric, as it did in the 1960s. All such discussions turn on the question of authority; not to be resolved in a sentence, but too many stupidities and cruelties have been committed in its name.

In Sydney I met the Tasmanian writer C. J. Koch, descendant of the redoubtable Captain Hurburgh, John

Mitchel's pilot, 'the little Carthaginian'. Koch has written novels set in Tasmania, and politely agreed with some of my wilder impressions of the island, of the people and their character, even their appearance; or at least he understood how the impression had been received. He has a passion for the place, and called elegant Sydney 'this whore of a city'. (Sydney calls itself, I was told, 'the Gay capital of the universe'.) Sydney Opera House is more democratic, less assertive than it looks in photographs, where it seems to be sailing out flamboyantly on its own promontory. It is like a gigantic series of white whelk shells that snuggle down into their own landscape, townscape: Australian-polite.

In Sydney's Hyde Park I went into the Anzac Memorial. Australians greatly honour their war dead, and there were many; my trip had begun with a commemoration of them, Anzac Day. You mount broad steps and, inside, you look down into a balustraded well, on to a bronze of a naked, prone young man, by Raynor Hof. In the vaults below are photographs of another projected bronze figure by the same sculptor, of a woman, naked; not a virgin or a goddess, but a realistically naked woman, her arms round a crossbeam like a yoke, and she looks down at piles of realistically dead men, her sons, brothers, lovers. The figure was to be called 'The Crucifixion of Civilisation' but the Roman Catholic Archbishop of Sydney, Dr Sheehan (the Irish again), objected, on the grounds that it was a blasphemy to put a woman in the position of the Crucifixion. Also, his secretary explained, 'That a nude woman should be selected as a symbol of civilisation only renders such statuary the more objectionable. . . . A perfectly nude woman is immoral and revolting in a memorial like that.' It was never erected.

Could I bear to live in a country dominated in such a fashion by priests? Could I have lived in the Ireland created by Cullen? Perhaps; but priests should not have too much public power. No one should.

From Sydney I flew back to Gloucestershire, where I had moved from London in the early 1960s. I approved of many of the liberalisations of the period, and disliked some of the 'anarchies and nihilisms' as much as Cullen might have done. The power of fashion seemed too great at that time. Even people you knew would be all right one day and the next time you met them they were wearing robes and bells and saying, 'Do your own thing.' The trouble was, I doubted their rebel credentials; I suspected that many of them, at school, had been teacher's pets, friends with the screws, whereas I had been more or less permanently on the chain-gang. Then, as now, they were simply going with the tide.

I also disliked and feared the then current cult of Eastern religions. That one had respect for and interest in other cultures, and people from them, went without saying, but to devalue one's own tradition was dangerous. People who came to Britain should be invited inside its cultural tradition, it should be seen to have one worth joining, and within it, of course, they should retain whatever in their own was important to them. This, to a large extent, is what the Irish had done in Britain and in the colonies. That gave some chance of growth by augmentation. We could all change each other. But to pretend that other cultures were better, and contained spiritual mysteries ours did not, was reactionary rubbish, and dangerous for the future.

Even among those who did not go nearly so far, there seemed something seriously amiss. For a short time I earned my living as a fringe member of the television 'satire' boom. But if we were being 'subversive' in those programmes it was of a kind of class-authority that had already lost direction, was merely an imitation of its old self, without confidence. We were little boys sniggering, because the hitherto feared headmaster had lost his trousers. What authority were we going to replace this one with, when we had laughed it away? Some generalised social religion of 'love', without a god? No more than Somers, in D. H. Lawrence's *Kangaroo*, could I believe in that. One day after rehearsing a TV sketch, a time of companionship and laughter, when I was at last alone I burst into unexplained, un-accustomed tears, like the young Peter Conrad in Tasmania, sensing himself cut off from too much of what he valued. There can be Tasmanias of the spirit.

The 1960s consecrated the present. At that time I wanted to write a book that put the *past* in some sort of order, my past, which seemed the only way to celebrate another person's past, one whose life had ended in 1958, shortly before this new kind of present-tense life began. Sally's death had been a dis-connection, but the death and the life had contained signals which had to be kept in working order, maintained as a sequence with meaning, in the present.

This need for sequence is an attempt almost to conquer time; the past carried alive into the present. 'Authority', 'class', 'nationality', are words that shift meaning as fast as you write them. What matters is balance, within some form of living tradition, or so it seems to me now. Patrick had kept his balance, perhaps through evasiveness, but also (helped by his wife) within the tradition of Irish Catholicism. Henry Paul had kept his balance, helping to settle the new country he lived in, within the same tradition. My father's balancing-act in a world grown more complex was helped by an anarchic, or surreal, humour, but still inside the tradition. I felt grateful to them all; they had preserved for me a point to balance on.

Within tradition it will always be possible to detect the apparently absurd. If my heart sank, for example, at the stage-property nature of the hierarchy's vestments in the bishop's library in Auckland, it was encouraging to come across a poem on the subject by the American, Richard Wilbur.

The Rule
The oil for extreme unction must be blessed
On Maunday Thursday, so the rule has ruled,
And by the bishop of the diocese.

Does that revolt you? You are free
To squat beneath the deadly machineel,
That tree of caustic drops and fierce aspersion,
And fancy that you have escaped from mercy.
Things must be done in one way or another.

The danger lies in the fanaticism, the religious fundamental-
ism, that insists that things can only be done one way, and in no
other; Ireland, in the North, has already suffered enough from
that. But all things that tend towards good contain their
poison, 'their caustic drops and fierce aspersion', which can be
guarded against. To keep our dead alive within us is to keep
connection, keep sequence, alive; it is a sense of disconnection
that destroys us.

'Autobiography is traditionally a genre peculiar to the
upwardly mobile, the socially insecure, those who have no
context to explain them. Its purpose is to expunge pain, but
more than this, to create a life myth, an alternative support
system. In rewriting history and establishing causation a
measure of control over circumstances is achieved. It is a
daring and agonising task which may not fulfil its intended
purpose.'

It may not, and on the whole I go along with Anita
Brookner's remarks, except that I find it difficult to imagine
anyone feeling so perfectly 'in context' that they have no
explaining to do, if only to themselves. That anyone could feel
wholly at home and comfortable in the world is an unattractive
thought, to me.

Twenty-five years after writing that book I find I have been
at the same sort of thing again, 'establishing causation', trying
to put a larger past in some sort of order. Inside the attempt
was a modest hope to help diminish, somehow, the lack of
sympathy that still disfigures the relations of Britain with
Ireland, to re-examine the nature of 'Irishness' in order to
understand what benefits and confusions it has brought me

and others. The Irish are now doing so for themselves. A native writer, Seamus Deane, has said: 'Everything, including our politics and our literature, has to be re-written, i.e. re-read. This will enable new writing, new politics, unblemished by Irishness, but securely Irish.' Perhaps Irish-born writers of the new generation will be able to do this.

But the old resentments linger. After I came back from Australia I returned to Carlow, and bumped into Michael Purcell, of Carlow Heritage, by coincidence in Tullow Street. Under his arm he was carrying, framed, an old street-map of the town. No, Richard Paul's house had not been built there by 1798. No, the Croppie massacre would not have taken place in front of it – had it been there. They came past its site, along the road where I had seen Andrew Kavanagh running, but were allowed to go the length of the street, into the Potato Market, now a carpark, when the gates were shut on them and they were killed. 'It must have taken a long time,' said Purcell. 'There were no machine-guns in those days. The tale is that Bishop Keefe left open the gate of the seminary, [St Patrick's, where Father James Paul had studied] so that some of the boys could escape. Well, he didn't. It was locked. The church opened that gate thirty years later, on paper.'

True? Untrue? In Tullow Street still, a hundred years after, we hear the old Fenian suspicion of the church, of its political ambivalence. An eyewitness was Michael Farrell, but Purcell has his doubts about him too.

'He wrote it all down when everybody who could contradict him was dead. He was the only man to come back alive from interrogation at the barracks in Leighlin. He took a government job.'

'Not much of a job, surely. Gatekeeper of the asylum?'

'Oh, it was a good job, a government job.'

Was Farrell, too, 'a dobber', as perhaps was Martin Cash, another survivor, eyewitness of another kind of slow slaughter, on Norfolk Island?

Suspicions of the church, and suspicions of a man then who could take a government job: these can degenerate, as R. F. Foster says, into the concept of being 'more' or 'less' Irish than your neighbour and, as D. N. Doyle says, into 'a self-indulgent communal morbidity'. It would be good to think that such days are passing. 'If the claims of cultural maturity and a new European identity advanced by the 1970s can be substantiated,' says Foster, 'it may be by the hope of a more relaxed and inclusive definition of Irishness, and a less constricted view of Irish history.'

I would hope for that, and hope to be included in some way; so long as it did not mean too great a diminution of Irish identity. Trouble, and generations, have gone to the preservation of such Irishness as I and others like me possess. Like Jewishness, it would be a waste to throw it away.

Having asked so many questions, I find some have been answered merely by the asking of them. I feel my attic is in better order, and, if I should pick up something in it and still be puzzled, at least I will have some idea how it came there. We all have different paths, or should have. To feel a stranger and yet feel at home, as I do in England, is right for the human spirit. It would be no sort of life if we felt entirely comfortable in it.

Index

NOTE. P.J.Kavanagh is abbreviated to PJK, and Patrick Kavanagh (his great-grandfather) to PK.